Felix Cavaliere
Memoir of a Rascal

Written by Felix Cavaliere

With Mitch Steinman

COVER PHOTO: © 1967 Paul McCartney / Photographer: Linda
Credit: McCartney. All rights reserved.

Copyright © 2022 All Rights Reserved

The author has tried to recreate events, locales and conversations from memories of them. The author may have changed some identifying characteristics and details such as physical properties, occupations and places of residence.

Although the author has made every effort to ensure that the information in this book was correct at press time, the author does not assume and hereby disclaims any liability to any party for any loss, damage, or disruption caused by errors or omissions, whether such errors or omissions result from negligence, accident, or any other cause.

Dedication:

This is dedicated to the ones I Love
Dr. Felix V. and Laura Cavaliere. Parents who loved and cared.
To my children Aria, Laura, Christina, and Lisa who love and inspire.
To my dear wife, Donna, who loves and is always there for me.
My sister, Frances Bianchini, who loves and worries.
To my guru Swami Satchidananda who loved and guided.
And to "you", never feel left out.

PHOTO CREDITS

Frances Bianchini
Donna Cavaliere
Christina Cavaliere
John Howard
Gene Cornish
Aria Cavaliere
Liz Cruse
Obi Steinman
Benny Harrison

COVER PHOTO:　© 1967 Paul McCartney / Photographer: Linda
Credit:　McCartney. All rights reserved.

Contents

Foreword by Bruce, "Cousin Brucie" Morrow 6
Chapter 1: Pelham, NY 9
Chapter 2: The Rascals 37
Chapter 3: The Atlantic Years 50
Chapter 4: Writing the Songs 71
Chapter 5: Adventures and Misadventures 89
Chapter 6: Swami Satchidananda 160
Chapter 7: Paying if Forward 182
Chapter 8: The Rascals Breakup 191
Chapter 9: The Hall of Fame 211
Chapter 10: On Stage Once More 223
Chapter 11: Today and Tomorrow 241

Foreword by Bruce, "Cousin Brucie" Morrow

THE MUSKRAT RUMBLE (or how I was "kidnapped" by a bunch of Rascals)

My first get-together with Felix and the boys was quite unusual. It was a meeting that would last a lifetime. It started with a telephone call (remember those primitive devices) from their manager, Sid Bernstein. He enthusiastically said, "Bruce-kah (he always called me Bruce-kah), I think I have a hit. I'm managing a new New York group. We have a HOT record that I want you to play and break in New York." He told me about the "Young Rascals" and that they would pick me up after I finished my WABC Radio show." I protested that I was tired. Sid didn't hear me. I said goodnight to my audience, when four young men (assorted sizes) rushed into my studio, shoved a large muskrat fur coat over me and said, "Cousin Brucie, we are The Young Rascals, and you are our guest at the Phone Booth. We are going to introduce our new single. We're scheduled to go on at eleven, so let's move!"

The Phone Booth was a popular club in Manhattan. Guests would sit at tables or booths. Each sitting area would have a telephone - and there would be communication between tables. "Hello, can I buy you a drink" or "Could you get rid of that guy - I'd like to meet you?" It was a good idea for meeting (again before the internet - so analogue, but it worked). That's' how I met the "Young Rascals," by being willfully Cousin-napped. It was show time at the Booth and the MC yelped," Here's a new group of locals boys destined to become stars." The "Cousin-nappers" energetically came on stage. They were dressed in what was to become their early trademark costumes. These local boys now all looked like Lord Fauntleroy, wearing fancy shirts, jackets and "knickers." These knickers (trousers) were bloused and puffed over their buckled shoes. For some reason, they looked cute, not strange.

Felix introduced the group and said, "Here's our new hit record." I do not believe that the song was played on the air yet; however, what's a few more days? They performed "Good Lovin'." The audience was theirs and I was captured. The night was a huge success. The following evening, I played "the Hit" five or six times. The telephones lit up and the audience wanted more. The record stores (yes, we had record stores back then) quickly listed "Good Lovin'" as the top selling record of the week. The boys were on their way.

Felix Cavaliere always captured the spotlight. He was magic right from the beginning. His amazing natural talent on the keys of the Hammond B-3 and his powerful R&B vocals assured the band of an amazing career. Felix, Eddie Brigati, Dino Danelli and Gene Cornish grew very quickly to become America's Band during the decade. By 1968 they decided that they were much too mature to be called "The Young Rascals" so they dropped the "Young"- They were now "The Rascals" (older and much wiser).

Cousins, fast forward to June 27, 2017. There was Felix on my Palisades Park Reunion V show stage. Now he is solo Felix. Alone, but when I cued him to go on the air—it seemed and sounded like he was surrounded by an orchestra. He has that star magic of being able to fill a room all by himself. The audience at the live event, as well as my Sirius XM listeners, once again were captured by this man's talent, energy and charm. The standing ovations proved that this artist, this poet continues to deliver delicious music to his audience.

I always look forward to Felix's growth and ability to deliver "the goods." He was and is a National Treasure. And now Dear Cousins, let's find out a little more about this beloved friend. Open the pages carefully and get ready to discover the makings of a Star. Thank you, Cousin Felix.

Bruce "Cousin Brucie" Morrow

Chapter 1: Pelham, NY

Pelham Junior High, this kid I never saw before stood in front of me in line—his name was John Calagna. "Do you like rock and roll?" he asked me.

Rock and what? I had no idea what he was talking about. Little did he know that I'd spent the past 8 years of my life fingers deep in Bach, Beethoven, Schubert, and Chopin. With that said, I sure as hell didn't want to say anything that would cause me not to look cool. So, I said, "Sure." Then, I went home and turned on the radio.

What I heard that day I'll never forget. All of a sudden, I heard piano players playing like I'd never heard in my life: Ray Charles, Fats Domino, Jerry Lee Lewis, Allen Toussaint. Boogie Woogie, the sound was alien, and I've felt at home on that planet everyday ever since. Their raucous rhythms took hold of me and have never let go. Rock and roll may have been born in Cleveland, but for me, it was raised in New York with disc jockey Alan Freed spinning for WINS radio.

Ray Charles. I thought to myself, wow, he plays piano. And I play piano. Maybe I could play like that. It really hit me. The sound I heard that day coming out of my parents' radio was certainly nothing like the classical music I'd play every Friday on a little make-shift stage in my music teacher's home.

Fortunately, I had a cousin on my mother's side who showed me how to play boogie-woogie with the left hand and I suddenly realized I could use that as the basis to play anything, including covers of most of the songs on the radio. In the ninth grade some guys had a band they called the "Swingin' 6" and needed a piano player. They asked me if I'd join, and I did. We'd play standards, like at weddings, parties, school dances or wherever. And sometimes, somewhere in the middle, when the adults didn't notice, we'd sneak in some Little Richard or Fats Domino for the teenagers. Later, in high school, I put together a singing group, a mixed group of black and white kids and we'd do covers of these great little songs by groups like the Drifters. We'd enter talent shows and win every year.

It was so special in those days. We were just kids playing for other kids and sharing our own kind of music, different, a world removed from the music our parents listened to. Our music was the thread that brought us together. It poured out of the radio and off the record store shelves. I'd save money and hit the record stores, ransacking the bins in search of the sounds that stood out for me. Often it was the R&B tracks of black artists that lit me most intensely. That's actually how I found "Good Lovin,'" an R&B song by a black group named the Olympics. You couldn't hear a lot of black acts on the radio because the big New York stations like WABC didn't play them. But they were on the shelves, and you could find them if you knew where to look. And when you'd find them, take them home and put the needle down, you'd find joy.

Pure joy! That's what I heard. That's what I still hear when I listen to those artists. Ray Charles was one of the first who really moved me. Listening to 'What'd I Say' blew me away. Years later I'd meet him, but back then he was this voice that just kept sticking in my head; it was the coolest, sweetest, most emotional sound. I didn't know then that the sound I heard as joy came from a recipe mixed with so much more. This wasn't the Beethoven, Mozart or Chopin my piano teacher taught me to play with precision; it was loose, soulful. It spoke to me in a language beyond words.

Mrs. Laura Cavaliere was the most determined and loving mom a kid could ever ask for. She wanted her children to succeed and, if that meant rounding them up when it was time to quit playing and start learning, well, then so be it. As a kid in Pelham Manor, New York, like most of my friends, I wanted to play baseball. We'd set up games of street ball, where the bases were manhole covers and what we used as a bat was really more of a stick. My mom knew when it was time for the game to end. That would be at the exact time my piano lessons were about to begin. She had a pretty unique way of getting us to the ninth inning. "Here she comes," one of the neighborhood kids would yell. And, sure enough, down the street came mom, driving the family car onto our baseball "field." You know what—it's hard to play baseball without bases, something my mother knew. She'd drive the car right up and on top of the manhole cover that stood in for home plate.

She didn't have to say, "it's time for you to practice, Felix." I knew it as soon as I saw the car coming. She wasn't kidding around. Three lessons a week, two at home plus practice and another at the nearby music academy, the Allaire School of Music. Beethoven, Mozart, all the masters.

There would be no Willie Mays or Mickey Mantle for her son. Who knew—I sure didn't—that one day in a far-off universe the great Willie Mays would ask Laura Cavaliere's son to autograph a 45 rpm record with the rock group's name "The Rascals" on the label?

All I knew was that I wanted to be outside, on the street, not inside pecking away at a piano. Baseball was a huge interest for me, then, as it is now. But I had to be realistic. Here I was a short Italian kid—about one foot tall with a lazy eye from birth and the name Felix. What chance did I have? It's not exactly the path to the Hall of Fame, though one day I would be in one, just not that one.

Self-confidence was something I had to develop. I was born cross-eyed and had an eye operation when I was five years old. That meant I had to wear a patch on one eye. It was hard for me to be socially comfortable. I got to know what it was like to be bullied, something that's stuck with me my whole life. One day I got so ticked off at the other kids laughing at me that I tore the patch off. My vision never really got developed in that eye, but, fortunately, I had a good ear— especially for music. I didn't know then that music would become my life and my livelihood, that one day it would take me on a journey around this beautiful country of ours, and all over the world, meeting and becoming friends with some of my own childhood heroes, both in music, baseball and world leaders. It's a journey that's lasted over a half-century. And it all began with those music lessons in my parents' parlor back in Pelham, New York.

The music lessons were just a part of my growing up as a kid in the 50's. My parents worked hard to make so much of me and my sister's early life happy and content. Part of that was moving us from the Bronx to a great neighborhood in West Chester County. They not only introduced me and my sister, Frances, to music at an early age, but they did everything to give us a comfortable upbringing. Pelham—my sister still likes to call it Pelham Manor, a smaller part of the larger town—was a place that gave us exceptional educational opportunities we wouldn't have had back in the city, or so our parents thought. Both our mom and dad were highly educated—our dad a dentist, our mom a pharmacist. Because of that, it was expected we would follow the same path— They had decided that I would become a doctor.

We were a tight-knit Italian family and if you're Italian you already know what that means. If you're not, well let's say a lot of relatives, a lot of food, and a lot of love. My mom's family came from Sicily. They grew wheat, but when a fungus affected the crop, my grandfather decided to relocate to America. That family, on my mom's side, was magical. What they accomplished here in America in terms of the medical profession was phenomenal. I'm so proud of my Italian roots, something I'll talk more about later, but, like most kids, I didn't get the full impact on me at the time. My father's people were from Naples. My name, Felix, goes back to St. Felix. I'm the third one in my lineage, after my father, Felix Cavaliere II, and grandfather; the three of us named for the patron saint of my ancestors' native village.

Being Italian in those days, in that neighborhood was both a blessing and a curse. It was very difficult for me to be socially comfortable or interact with others until the music came along. It allowed me to feel first-hand what it's like to be bullied and discriminated against. What it's like to be the outsider, wherever you happen to be, and whoever you are. It's something that too many of us have dealt, and unfortunately continue to deal with.

Discriminated against for being short, Italian, having a different name, being the guy with the long hair—whatever it was that made me different also gave me a bond with others sharing the same seat. It would creep into a lot of my decision-making, about music, about songwriting, really about life. It began with my mother, the most loving and most demanding person I knew. She demanded a lot of my sister and me because she loved us, and because she loved us, she had expectations for us.

Mom always set a good example for her kids. When we first moved to Pelham, she wanted to become a part of the community in any way she could. She was told she could serve the food. Here she was, a pharmacist, a woman of culture, told that she could serve the food. It is such memories that shaped my attitude toward rebelliousness.

Like my father who was denied membership into the Pelham Country Club because Italians, Jews, Hispanics, and Blacks were not allowed in. That hurt. It probably hurt me more than it hurt them, but I'm sure it hurt. And I never forgot it.

My parents carried on for the sake of their kids and their family, like so many of that generation. They each had their "roles." My mom was so many things in our family; she was not only the "designated driver," getting me back and forth to my piano lessons; she was also a devout Catholic and the churchgoing half of our parents, delivering my sister and me to mass every Sunday. She was always around priests and nuns. As I say, she was extremely Catholic. The nuns and sisters were around us all the time because the hospitals she worked in were Catholic hospitals. The nuns were like members of our family, so I was comfortable around them.

The one thing both mom and dad instilled in both my sister and me was a respect for education and a love of learning. To this day, I read everything I can get my hands on. You can find me in a bookstore anyplace I play. It was a huge sacrifice for our parents to make that move to Pelham Manor, but they made it because they wanted me and my sister to get a good education. They weren't rich, but they knew that real wealth was in what you knew, not what you had in the bank. There weren't many kids at that time, or probably now, who had a library in their homes, but we did. If we had a question about something for homework, we didn't have to go to the public library because we had one right there in the house. "Go look it up," is what our parents would tell us.

I didn't see a whole lot of my father as like so many dads in those days, he worked ungodly hours to provide for his family. The man was strict, stoic and tirelessly dedicated to his patients and that dedication also taught a lesson of hard work and the importance of doing what you love.

Truthfully, growing up I really didn't know him all that well. He served in the army during the war, and I can remember when he came through the door when back home, he had his army uniform on, I really didn't know who he was. He went in as a captain and was stationed in Hawaii, a place where, as an adult, I was able to return with him many years later, in the 1960's. It's one of my fondest memories of being with my dad. For one thing, he was amazed by the changes in the 20 years since the war. When he had served on the island, there was only one hotel! That really hit him, in terms of how much change had occurred. If you think about it, in those 20 years a lot of things changed in America, including the family structure.

Like I said, the parenting roles in our home were pretty well defined. Traditionally, in Italian families, like mine, the fathers went to work, and the mothers cooked the food. The difference in my family was that mom was also a professional woman, kind of a rare thing in those days. Both our parents were hard workers and good providers, but my mom was more of the constant presence in my childhood. There was probably a good reason why she pretty much doted on me. I know now that they had tried a long time to have a son; three miscarriages later, in 1942, I was born. My mother, I always tell people, made sure my feet never touched the ground. It was like she worried that something would happen to me, the son she'd wanted all her life. Between school, music lessons, and the occasional stick ball game, I had all a kid could want.

Our parents were happily married and really kind of the yin and yang to each other--my mother being the emotional one and my dad the more stoic. They complemented one another perfectly, giving both my sister and me fine role models for how couples should treat each other. Though he would never say it out loud, my dad really worshipped our mom.

They met at St. Vincent Hospital, where mom worked in the pharmacy. Dad went there one day to get some peroxide for one of his dental patients. He noticed her right away, especially when she gave him "extra" supplies. He kind of figured she liked him! He was right. They were married a short time later and tried to begin a family. Unfortunately, mom had a negative blood type that contributed, as I said, to several miscarriages, all of which made my eventual arrival as the only son truly special, as it is in most Italian families. That Italian heritage was always front and center growing up.

Italians pride themselves on having tight knit family structures, and mine was no different. My dad was the youngest in his family and had a sister, my aunt Emma, and a brother, my uncle Mike, who was a butcher. In those days, everyone in the family went to work, saved up their money and put it into a savings account. That account became the money needed to put dad through dental school. The whole family agreed that the money would be well spent on his education, and he never forgot that. Many years later, when he was a successful dentist, dad bought both his siblings houses. They were never far away from us, and my Aunt Emma even lived just two doors down from his office. My grandfather—dad's dad—was a barber down on Wall Street and cut the hair of a lot of people who really knew how to make money. When they gave him a tip, they really gave him a TIP—as in where putting his money would make him the most money, allowing him to do well, financially. I can't stress enough that my mother's side was and still is extremely accomplished. The genius level that was in that family is amazing. I'm still in touch with so many of them and meet new relatives all the time. When I did a show in Westbury, New York a while ago, I met about 18 relatives I didn't even know I had. Mom's family name is DiGiorgi and it's a huge Italian family, really huge. I couldn't believe the number of people.

Having a television set, black and white, of course was a big deal during my childhood, and it opened our world to shows like Sid Caesar, Milton Berle, Howdy Doody, and Steve Allen. I loved Steve Allen; he was the first host of the "Tonight Show" and made a deep impression on me as a kid. The first time I could envision myself being on TV was when I saw Elvis Presley. There was that whole thing where they wouldn't show him below the waist because it might drive the girls crazy. I thought to myself, "This looks like fun. I could enjoy doing this."

It wasn't the first or last time I saw rock and roll as a way of getting noticed by girls. Adding to the Elvis allure was the fact he didn't wear a suit. Everybody who sang at that time wore a suit, people like Frank

Sinatra, Perry Como, all those singers who our parents listened to on the radio or their record players. Elvis didn't wear a suit and that, in addition to the music, made him somehow more "real" to me. Besides all the entertainment on TV, there was, of course, Walter Cronkite doing the evening news and that, especially, opened up my eyes to the world beyond Pelham Manor.

There were so many ways in which our parents exposed my sister and me to horizons beyond our own neighborhood. I believe it was important to our parents that we see more of the world than we could see from our bedroom windows. I remember going to Quebec, Bermuda, Virginia Beach, Miami Beach. We never really called it a "vacation." For most of the people from that generation, all they knew how to do was work. When mom and dad did take time off to travel with my sister and me, it was considered more a "family trip," a time to see new things and places and learn from them—kind of like an extension of our formal learning in school. What I don't think either of our parents counted on was that school would be the place where I'd be introduced to this thing called rock and roll. All that exposure to people like Elvis on our television screen was spilling out onto the street and into the school yard and that is where my foray into rock and roll really began.

Rock and roll also caused me a fair number of problems, especially when it came to what my parents—my father especially—planned for my future. Those plans didn't involve playing in night clubs and making records. That was never in the cards. It was always expected that I would go to college and, eventually, medical school to become a doctor. My dad worked tirelessly, but he loved being a dentist. Between his medical degree and my mom's pharmacy degree, my future was set. It had long been decided. I would go to Syracuse University, study pre-med, move forward from there and become the doctor I was meant to be. Medicine was in our family; it was in my blood. Medicine not music, was the family goal. Music was a pastime; medicine was a profession. There was no cure, however, for what I was about to experience in my young life.

My love of music came from my mom of which I'm so very thankful. Laura Cavaliere played a beautiful piano, and her love became my love.

Laura Cavaliere died of cancer on my thirteenth birthday.

On the brink of everything in life—high school, college, career, when suddenly the life of someone who is so important is taken away. My mother's death left my dad a single father and it left me, a young teenager, questioning a lot of things about life, starting with God and the value of religion. It threw me for a loop. As a child, it really didn't make sense that someone so good, so young, would just be plucked from this world in the prime of her life.

I didn't get it. My mother had led a very spiritual life. Dad would only go into a church if it was raining; it was mom who would drive my sister and me to church on Sundays. Sometimes we'd even attend mass during the week. Mom was a devoted believer. There was a part of me that couldn't reconcile her goodness with her early death. She was only 45 and I was very, very affected by her passing. She died in our house, and it wasn't a peaceful ending. My sister, Fran, recalls her flailing her arms in the bed and we were both very scared by the words she said: "My poor children. My poor children." I really withdrew after that. I had no place to put my grief in the immediate aftermath of my mother's death.

I needed someone to talk to. There was a great priest in our town who tried to help me, but then he got transferred to another parish, so I began a kind of search for answers. My dad couldn't help. All he did was throw himself into his work. When my mother passed, he was completely wrecked. A wreckage that he was never truly able to walk away from.

In time, it was the spirituality instilled in me by my mother that helped get me through her passing. I feel bad for people who believe in nothing. It's tempting when you lose someone who's so important to you. When you get your tail beat. It's good to have someplace to go for answers, to find a place that brings you light in your time of need. I think it's very important for people to have a path in life. There are many paths, not one, but any path is better than no path. And, as I've grown older, I see a lot of those paths converging and leading to the light.

At 13, I was just a kid who had only known, up to that point, all the joys of life. Just the year before, my mom had seen me play in a piano competition at Carnegie Hall; it was one of the last things she attended before the illness took over. The swift ending to such a wonderful life made me retreat into myself, hiding my feelings. Some part of me didn't want my father to see my sadness because I didn't want to make him sad. I became, in many ways, very serene, putting my grief into my music, but a different kind of music. It was music that helped me channel that grief and music that, ultimately, took me off the path of medicine and toward a very different destiny.

By the age of fourteen, I channeled a lot of my sadness into the band I'd started in school, the 'Swingin' Six.' Back then, I played guitar as well as piano. We were all in junior high and played just about everything that was "old" at the time, but we began to gradually throw in some newer rock. We'd play weddings, parties, school dances, anywhere we could. The next year, at 15, it was a singing group called "The Stereos." I didn't think anything of it at the time, but this, too, was a mixed-race singing group—black and white—like my earlier group. We'd play dances, talent shows where I started to sing as well as play and we won everything a group could win.

The rock and roll that Alan Freed had brought to New York continued to give me energy. I was getting better at using that left-hand boogie-woogie style my cousin taught me to learn more and more Little Richard and Fats Domino tunes. Songs that everybody knew. It really freed me up. After my mother passed, the pressure was off to play classical music, though. Don't get me wrong. I love the classics, but I was happy to be able to branch out. My dad really had no idea what I was doing. Soon, though, my piano teacher would know, oh, would she know!

My sister, Fran, remembers how that solemn British lady, Mrs. Eloise Close, first found out about my foray into rock and roll. During one of our lessons, I went into an upbeat boogie-woogie rock and roll tune. As

Fran recalls it, Mrs. Close did not see it coming and she very nearly passed out! That was nothing compared to the reaction my father was about to have. I didn't know it at the time, but I was on the brink of creating a family crisis that would bring me to a reckoning not only with my dad but my grandmother as well. Both not only wanted but insisted that young Felix was going to college—Syracuse University—and do the family name proud.

I was college-bound and my music was coming with me. The entire university was jamming within the world of R&B and Rock N Roll. I spent weekends entertaining a hungry student body and weeknights bonding with athletes who began gravitating to our music, and my fraternity brothers at SIGMA PHI EPSILON.

The Syracuse football team had won the National Championship the year before, going undefeated. There's an unrivaled energy that exists in a university housing the #1 football team in America, and the atmosphere on the campus of Syracuse University was nothing short of electric. Jim Brown had just left to join the Cleveland Browns where he would become the greatest running back of his day, and yet the school didn't skip a beat with Ernie Davis running the ball in his place. Ernie grew up in Elmira, NY, just a couple hundred miles from Pelham.

Ernie Davis became the first African American to win the Heisman Trophy. My memory of Ernie was that of a young man who carried his smile with even more confidence and assurance than he did the football. He was a great kid who made the University proud! Ernie was the first player drafted in the 1962 NFL draft. I cried when I heard the news shortly thereafter that Ernie had been diagnosed with Leukemia and became downright heartbroken upon learning of his death a year later at the age of twenty-three.

The musical side of my life at Syracuse was fueled by two things. First, I worked at the college radio station, where I'd hear all the latest rock and roll releases and learn a lot from them. The bug bit me again and just kept on biting. It's really where my music career started to take off. Because Syracuse U. had so many frats there was always someplace for a band to work. Some of my fraternity brothers asked me to be in a group, which soon became "Felix and the Escorts." We made a record; side A was a song I wrote titled "The Syracuse." A fun catchy tune incorporating the names of various college campuses. The other side was a cover of the Laverne Baker song "I Am Saved." Although the record was only played locally, it made a big splash upon the student body who began seeking out our performances every Friday and Saturday night. I wasn't the only one in the group who got his start there. The bass player, Mike Esposito, eventually became a part of the '60's group the Blues Magoos. We got a pretty good following but playing the frats every Friday and Saturday night means your academics are going to suffer. That's one thing that happened. The other was that I went to Syracuse to be pre-med, based on what I saw as a dedication to healing that I learned from my dad. Truthfully, I didn't find that in the courses I was taking—biology, chemistry, all those courses that you had to take in order to get into med school just didn't interest me. I also saw seniors who spent four years of their lives who didn't get admitted into medical school and that seemed like a waste to me.

Back then, studying music in college really didn't seem like much of an option, because the courses were more historical, rather than creative. Syracuse had its share of future rock stars, one of them being Lou Reed who was a student there at the same time. He was in my graduating class; we didn't know each other well, although we both knew of each other. In those days, he was really a very erudite person, very thoughtful, and very much like what you might have called a beatnik back then, which would probably describe a lot of us.

In the summer of 1963, Felix and the Escorts were offered a gig at the Raleigh Hotel in the Catskill Mountains, a resort that believe it or not, is still there today. Our drummer had connections with Jules Styne, a composer of Broadway hits such as Gentlemen Prefer Blondes and Funny Girl. Mr. Styne had connections with the owners of the hotel. He got us an audition for what they called the swing band that played for the soon-to- be retiring guests, however we also got to play for the teenagers by the swimming pool and in the lounge. The gig paid $60 a week, including room and board— a lot of money in those days. I thought I'd died and gone to heaven. It turned out to be a great summer that dramatically changed the course of my life.

Every weekend, a star performer, sometimes a comedian, sometimes a pop group, would come in and headline. One weekend the headliners were Joey Dee and the Starliters, a year or so removed from their hit 'The

Peppermint Twist.' Among Joey Dee's band was a player named David Brigati, the older brother to Eddie who in a short time would become the Rascal's frontman. Needless to say, that playing on the same venue that weekend would have a pretty profound effect on my life.

The success of that summer both internally and externally was such that I couldn't see myself going back to school. A four-year degree is intensified tenfold when it's attached to graduating into med school. Having the majority of my focus attached to playing music live, getting lost in the vibe of celebration had seriously begun to infringe upon all my desires to put in the work necessary to continue on track towards med school.

I hadn't seen a lot of my dad during those first years at Syracuse although he did come out to the Catskills one weekend to spend a little time. There's a pull, a gravity force that many fathers have over their children and for me, that pull was my father's dream of me becoming a doctor. While a father's dream isn't necessarily a mandate, there is this essence of responsibility as one begins to grapple over the choice between breaking the dreams your parents have created on what they believe is in your best interest.

It's that dream of my father's that I was struggling with so deeply throughout the weekend of his trip to the Catskills. It wasn't so much his permission that I was seeking as much as it was his acceptance. I didn't want to let him down, and yet I couldn't simply ignore my dreams any longer. I was struggling over the thought of causing him pain.

Sitting alone in the coffee shop on the eve of my father's arrival, the maître d' of the club must have seen something in my demeanor as he approached and began talking to me. We spoke for a little while which at the time only seemed to add even more fuel to my fire as he went out of his way to let me know that I'd be crazy to go back to school. "You're blind if can't see the reaction you're getting when you play. You're good and trust me, this is what you're meant to be doing."

My father wasn't a nightclub kind of guy. But I was hoping that he'd see something in my playing, the crowd's response that might help make my conversation with him a bit more palatable. Wishful thinking perhaps, but anything to help grease the wheels.

It was the following evening when I witnessed this maître d'—for the most part a complete stranger—give me one of the great assists of my young life. I watched as he poured on the schmooze the moment my father entered the ballroom. Front row seats. Best table in the dining room. Everything. The man continued to rave about me to my father throughout the evening, acting like I was Elvis Presley, and he was Elvis' father. My father was very old-fashioned. Still, when he saw how people treated me and looked up to him because he was my father, it made a real difference. My dad was blown away. You may even say he was primed.

On top of that, I had this little blue notebook where I wrote down everybody I met, their names, phone numbers, everything. People would tell me to look them up when I came to New York. Maybe it was to show off to their dates. I don't know, but I kept it and between the compliments he heard others give me and the names I kept in that notebook, my father was increasingly convinced. "You seem to be doing pretty good up here," he said to me.

"I'm making $60 a week," I said proudly. He smiled and I was on my way. That night meant a lot to me.

So, I used that night to tell dad I wanted to go into music, not medicine. We struck a deal, but before the deal was final he told me, in no uncertain terms, "no son of mine is going to be a bum." It really shook up the family. My grandmother even tried to bribe me into returning to Syracuse by promising to buy me a new car. Still, the deal between dad and me was struck with a handshake. "Try it for a year," he said. "And if it doesn't work out, promise you'll go back to school." He gave me his blessing and I gave him my promise. I owe my dad that and so much more. At one point, he bankrolled me to buy my first Hammond organ. It wasn't the now famous B-3 which I play today, but a smaller version, the Hammond M-3. He loaned me the $700 to buy it and I'd like to think that he felt extreme pride in both of us every time he saw me on television sitting behind my Hammond in love with every second of every performance.

With my father's blessing secured and with a great deal of optimism and hope, I packed up and went to New York along with the other guys in the band. We all took off like a shot at the end of summer to make it big in the city. So here we are in New York, with no work, a lot of promises, but no work. Here's the thing that so many fresh-faced fellow dreamers come to realize about New York City. New York gives you the opportunity to make it, but it doesn't give you a helping hand. It says okay, you've made it here; now it's up to you to make it here.

It wasn't long, a couple months at the most before our parents began to rumble. "You know what? We're not paying for you guys to be bums." Back to school was pretty much what we were all hearing. Things didn't look good as one by one the first couple of bandmates headed back to the comfort of their frat house.

It seemed that I received the call just as I had begun packing my bags as well. It was Saturday afternoon when a call came from Don Davis, who was Joey Dee's manager. Joey and the Starliters were playing in Europe and their organist, recently married, quit and headed home to the U.S. to reunite with his newlywed. Joey needed a replacement, and I needed to be there by Monday if I wanted the gig.

I landed in Frankfurt, Germany two days later and began the opening chapter to what I call my own "magical mystery tour."

Joey Dee was a big star throughout Europe, and here I was, not even twenty-one, preparing to tour the continent as a member of the Starliters.

No one to meet me at the airport. All I had was a phone number to the army base where Joey and the group were staying. No address, no contacts, just a phone number. Problem was I didn't even know how to use a German telephone. Instead of getting a dial tone after you put the coins in, you get three beeps. I had no clue at the time that that was their dial tone.

It was David Brigati, Eddie's older brother who finally answered the phone. "What are you doing here?" he asked, having no clue that I was coming.

"I'm here because I'm supposed to be your organ player."

"Okay, but be careful when you come here," he said. "We had a little situation between one of our band members and a soldier's wife, it's a little ugly at the moment."

So, I got in a cab and headed straight for the tense army base. Great… however, my mind was quickly distracted by the events taking place outside the taxi's window. There was some kind ceremony overtaking the city. I came to learn that it was a yearly event that overtakes the entire country along with Switzerland and Austria called Fasching. Colorful costumes of the sort we wouldn't see in America for a few more years. Loud Bavarian music and over the top parades and celebrations around every corner. It was almost as scary as it was fascinating. Part of me thought about the comforting confines of Syracuse.

New blood. I was hit up immediately by a few dudes in the band. Attacked like a college kid who actually had a few bucks in his pockets. It startled the hell out of me; here were these professional musicians scraping by to the point where they needed to hit me up for cash. I thought it was strange that David Brigati was making the same amount of money for a week's work as I was being paid, and he'd been with Joey for years

Fat Frankie was our road manager. When things got boring, the guys in the band would pour talcum powder all over his mattress and when Frankie plopped himself onto it, the powder would go up in a puff of smoke and everybody thought it was hilarious. Every night I'd come out of the dressing room in a shirt with pockets and every night David would rip the pockets off. After the fourth or fifth night, David informed me, "You don't wear pockets on stage, get it?"

What did I get myself into? This kind of stuff went on all the time, whether out of boredom or just the result of guys having too much time on their hands. It was as if there wasn't an adult in the room. I definitely didn't consider myself above the hijinks, but there's no doubt looking back that I was so utterly focused on making this a career that I missed so much of the periphery. But all that changed in one evening.

The crowd was normally a tad subdued through most of the performances by bands opening for us, however, that night the crowd began going crazy. It was so unusual that I had to take a look. It was my first peek at the band that would be known worldwide as the Fab Four in less than a year. And yet, here they were, unknowns throughout most of the globe—months away from the release of Love Me Do—creating a fandemonium. Their mop tops, considered long hair at the time, bouncing to the backbeat. My biggest takeaway of that evening was how crazed the crowd got whenever they'd play one of their songs. Even in those early days before Beatlemania made it's splash you could barely hear their voices over the screaming. Every night the audience went absolutely berserk. There was some magic in there. They weren't yet the great musicians they'd become, but there was something there. It was cool. These guys could sing, no doubt about that. Watching them perform, playing their instruments, singing, harmonizing… I knew I could do that. I knew I wanted to do that. Not only did it look like a lot of fun, with all the screaming females around, but I saw I could actually do this. It was not unattainable. When you're in college, you see a lot of people who are successful in business, but there seems to be a big jump between them and you. I didn't feel that when I saw the Beatles back then. It was actually possible for me to do this. They were the Beatles, but one day another little-known band named the Rascals would challenge them at the top of the music charts.

Years later Paul and I found ourselves sitting, reminiscing about those days and I remember him leaning back seemingly in awe of the memory, looking at me and stating with such wanderlust, "We were so young." And it hit me. He was so right. We weren't even twenty-one, and yet, we were beginning to travel the world on our own ventures. It was a magnificent time, our journeys still on the launching pad.

It was the opening. Man, I had a ball. Now I had a job, as well as a chance to see the world from an interesting perspective. What occurs to me now, more than anything else about that moment in time is how much I owe my mother for how far I had come. When you're playing classical music, you're playing music that's been around hundreds of years. Making me practice and learn the classics really gave me a perspective; it helped me realize that something I could create might actually last. Now, at that time, I had no idea that I was on a path to playing music that might also be around for at least a half-century. In the back of my mind, I was still this little guy who wasn't going to be good at sports, but I was building confidence. Between the crowd's response and the ladies who began seeking this shy American kid out after each performance, I began to visualize myself living within this dream I had envisioned.

I was having a great time. We traveled by train, which was an absolute brilliant way to take in the glory of Europe in the early '60s, less than twenty years removed from WWII. And although traveling by train was such a treat, the story behind it was eerie. Joey Dee and a few members of the band had become terrified of flying after the plane that took the lives of Buddy Holly, Richie Valens, and the Big Bopper crashed outside of Clear Lake, Iowa in the dead of winter 1959. Turns out he and the band were on that same plane just a few weeks before.

The B-side to performing on stage, traveling with a band, and living this strange, surreal life on the road is the call toward narcotics. It was an immediate eye-opener the role that drugs played in this biosphere. And although the most prominent drug of the day was pot, this being the early '60s, it was considered illegal, and in many corners of America, an illicit narcotic. And those that partook would go through great lengths and creative methods to stash their stash.

Here I was, working for a guy who wouldn't fly, and getting a little nervous about the lifestyle surrounding me. My roommate when I was working with Joey was Willie Davis, an old-school musician from the cotton fields of Georgia. Before I left for Europe, my dad had given me a bag filled with prescriptions for preventing colds, the flu, even headaches... seeing the bag, Willie said to me, "Hey little brother, what you got in the bag? Let me see that bag." Willie took everything in the bag, all the drugs and dumped them into a bowl before mixing it all into a few Kool cigarettes. The dude proceeded to light up and puff away. The powder from the drugs turned his whole mouth white. I'd never seen anything like it. Definitely not in Kansas anymore.

I began to envision the whole sound of what I was doing from Joey because he had also used an organ in the act as I did in the Catskills when he first heard me. He was the star, and I was a sideman. There's nothing like being a sideman when you start out in music. There's less pressure. You don't have to worry about anything. There's a sense of apprenticeship, an invaluable learning experience as there's so much beyond the music to deal with.

I had a vision, and it wasn't long before I found myself yearning to lead a band again. I knew it was time for me to branch out and find the best people available to form my own group. I continued on with Joey at his club, The Starliter, before taking a job in Las Vegas with a singer named Sandu Scott, all the while envisioning my sound.

Those of you around my age no doubt remembers what a huge deal the draft played in our lives. The possibility of being drafted put lives on hold, it hung over our heads like a threat. I wanted to start my own band but didn't feel it would be the right thing to do—to go ahead and start a band and then have to go into the service. That didn't make a lot of sense to me. So, I found myself back in the U.S. facing the very real possibility of being inducted into the armed services. America was in the middle of the Vietnam War and people my age were getting drafted in numbers far too large to ignore. Especially those who left school, as I'd done.

I was feeling a little disoriented, my life in a holding pattern and it was around this time when I began growing my hair and ingesting a little pot now and again continuing to get in touch with my inner artist.

I spent the night at my father's house in Pelham before reporting to the local draft board the next morning. I remember smoking a joint before getting on the bus, which dropped me off directly in front of the entrance into the induction center. I didn't know what to expect, but I went through the lines and got my eyes tested. "Hey, Ringo, your turn," one of the guys in charge called out to me. They brought me to a bench where three or four guys were sitting, all waiting to see the psychiatrist to be evaluated for duty. It had me recalling a story of two friends back in Pelham who were a little older. One of them decided he was going to travel to Hyannis Port, Massachusetts, steal a boat, and go down to Cuba and help Fidel with his revolution. Instead, he got drafted, showed up, and was immediately sent to a psychiatrist. Why? Maybe it had something to do with wanting to fight for Fidel. In any case, he told me he was found unfit to serve and sent home. Whether he ever went to Cuba, I don't know, but he sure as hell didn't go to Vietnam.

The shrink saw my hair, and I think he could see my state and I gathered he was starting to think my qualifications for duty were, shall we say, questionable. To be honest, he might have smelled the pot, too. I had a folder with a rubber band around it and was so nervous that I got my hand caught in the rubber band. In any case, the man in uniform stamped my file "unfit for duty" and sent me to another bench. A guy sitting there looks at me and says, "I got one kidney." I figured I'd been sent to the "right" bench: the one where those about to go home had been sent. I was right. I was released, along with all the others next to me on that bench. Suddenly, I thought "Oh, my God, I'm outta here.

After being found ineligible for the draft, I knew it was time. Now, finally, I could start the band. From my initial trip to Germany, my goal was to get the best musicians, guys who could not only play but sing. I was young, but I felt my vision was sound, and I had New York City as a drawing point. A city filled with great musicians everywhere you looked. The Joey Dee connection, begun in the Catskills, nurtured in Europe, and continuing at the Starliter proved fortuitous. With the help of fate, and good fortune, I was about to meet the three other people who would permanently alter the course of my life.

Chapter 2: The Rascals

Have you ever found yourself face-to-face with people you know are going to change your life, but you don't know it yet? That's where I found myself now that I was free of the draft and ready to start up my own band. The venue was the Choo Choo Club in Garfield, New Jersey, named after the fact the damn thing was built just feet off a set of tracks. It was like an earthquake every time a train choo chooed its ass past.

Eddie Brigati was always hanging around his big brother David who was an original member of Joey Dee's band. Eddie was a true New Jersey kid. Outgoing, cocky, a killer with the girls, and fun as hell. He would come and sit in with the band, and when he sang, he would blow away every other singer and then just walk off, just like that, just like the spoiled little brat that he was.

Whenever he was on stage, the crowd would yell, "Let the kid sing." Right from the start, he impressed me. He was funny as hell, a real wise ass. But there was something charming about the kid and everybody saw it. Eddie's voice was a gift; the sweetest singing voice… just sit back and listen to "How Can I Be Sure."

It was there at the Choo Choo Club that I asked Eddie to join the band that I wanted to put together.

At Joey Dee's Club, the "Starliter," there was a guitar player named Gene Cornish, who came in from Rochester as part of a band called "The Unbeatables." His group had a tough time making it in New York, so he was playing as part of the "Starliters." Gene was what I would call a "rockabilly nut." He was very naïve to the ways of the big city, but had a huge heart and, still today, just lives to play guitar. I figured he could play guitar in my new group, so I started to feel as if I was getting closer to having a full band—if the others agreed.

I was increasingly anxious to make the move and went about it carefully. It made me a little nervous. It was a huge step. At the time, I confided in Ruby Toy, a woman I was dating at the time. Joey's band would come out and open with a few songs before Joey took the stage. Well, one day, after seeing our warmup, Ruby was sitting near the bandstand; she could tell there was something on my mind and inquired about it. I told her I was a little depressed because I really wanted to be more out front, to have my own group again, as I'd had in college. I thought maybe Joey might let me sing a song during the show, along the lines of the warmup set we did before his entry. "There's no way Joey is going to let you sing," she told me. "You'd blow him away."

Ruby told me of a drummer who, in her words was a thousand times better than the drummers we were playing with. I was skeptical, honestly, I wasn't sure how tuned in she was as to what made a great drummer. She took me to a club called the Metropole, on 7th & 48th. It was a stage where you could see the musicians playing from the street. I didn't even go in.

Turns out she did know something about drummers, and she knew one of the best there was—and probably still is. I stood there and watched the drummer through the window. I watched him play two songs and I knew… this was the guy. Simply put, Dino Danelli was magnificent. He wasn't just sitting back keeping time, he was putting on a show. He was phenomenal, his hands so quick, his stage presence so captivating.

To this day, Dino is one of the most dynamic drummers ever. I approached him soon thereafter and made him an offer he couldn't refuse. There was no way I was going to let Dino slip through my hands. He was truly, in my mind, the last piece to the puzzle. I really felt like I'd found the best musicians in terms of singing and musicianship. To this day I know I was right.

Gene still labels what the four of us had back then as "totally magic"—and he's right. We all had something different, but, man, we all had something that each of us needed. Here I was, inspired by the great jazz guys like Jimmy Smith. I kind of had that in common with Dino. He played with and really thought of himself as a jazz guy, somebody in the vein of Gene Krupa—one of the great drummers of his era.

Eddie was a completely different kind of animal. Like I said, a total "Jersey guy." I think it's something in the water. I'd never met anyone like these guys. Take "Fat Frankie," Joey Dee's road manager. Frankie, who was aptly named, gave me one of my first tastes of "Jersey." First time I saw him, I was at the swimming pool at the Raleigh and a van pulled up. The door to the van opened, and a behemoth of a man says, "Okay, everybody outta the way." The thing is there was nobody in the way.

I remember that after Joey Dee's show, during the time I was playing the lounge, and Fat Frankie invites me backstage to meet Joey's group. I'm looking at these guys, and I'm watching Fat Frankie, and he's in a mirror admonishing the band. He's slicking back his hair, and he says to them, "You know what? You guys are stars, but I'm getting all the girls tonight, and you guys are going back to your fricking rooms." The next thing I see is two guys from Joey's band step up and rip Frankie's lapels as they lifted his jacket all the way up to his neck, telling him, "This is how the girls are going to see you tonight, Frankie." I'd never seen anything like it. It was the way people from Jersey interacted with each other.

It was really a different kind of life. In a lot of ways, in a smaller body, that huge Jersey personality was right there inside Eddie Brigati. This is what I had just entered into. This is how these guys were; there was no acting. I'm sure his deep-seated Italian roots also led Eddie to be very influenced by his family, especially his older brother. As much as I tried, as much as I wanted to be like a brother to Eddie, I never really could penetrate the wall that was his family, though we sure as hell clicked when it came to writing our own songs, eventually.

Although the four of us were completely different animals, the combination was perfect. Life-changing. Playing live forced us to perform songs that made people get up and move. These were clubs, not coffee houses. This was Rock N Roll and R&B not folk music. We started to get a real following, mainly by playing covers of other people's tunes, done our own way. Gene, these days, says that, looking back, we were like "a strange cover band." We didn't play the obvious covers that other bands played at that time. If we played a Beatles song, for example, it wouldn't be the obvious Beatles song. "Slow Down" is probably one of the better examples. The club owners loved us because when we played, people got up to dance. And the more they danced, the more they drank. And the more they drank, the more money the clubs made.

Club owners weren't crazy about slow tunes, so we'd mostly play fast and loud. One of the first songs that fit this bill was one I wrote titled "Come On Up." It was the kind of song the bar owners loved because it put people in a good mood and kept them going back to the bar. As one club owner told me, "You know what makes a good band? Look out there at those people dancing. They're going to get hot and then they're going to drink. And when they drink, they dance, and when they dance, they drink some more. A band that makes that happen is a good band."

Back then, all the club owners wanted were covers of songs people knew. I would listen closely to the radio for good songs that weren't necessarily hits—yet at least—but were on a record, so I could say to the club owners, "Hey, look, it's legit. I got it right here on a record." That's how we got to do "Good Lovin." I found it deep in a bin at one of the many record stores I'd frequent. Nobody wanted to hear your emotions or your own original songs in the clubs. Creativity wasn't the point. It was only about getting people up and moving. It actually turned out to be good for us because we might not have otherwise done "Good Lovin," or "Mustang Sally," or any one of a number of other songs I "discovered" back then in obscure record bins.

We needed a name, something that would stick. We kept playing around with different names, but none of them really seemed to work. Depending on who you listen to, the story is that Dino came up with the "Rascals" because he was up till 6am one night watching the "Little Rascals" on TV or that the comedian Soupy Sales, who was a huge act at the time, did. I prefer the Soupy Sales version. Soupy had a big TV show on WNEW in New York and all of us were fans. We were trying to get recognized, and Soupy had a hit record at the time called "The Mouse," kind of a novelty record. He was touring and everything. We thought, why not just go down to the station and introduce ourselves. Great idea, right? Well, it actually was.

We figured that since he was touring, maybe he'd let us be his backup band. We connected with him right away. He cracked us up with all his jokes. He was an extremely talented guy and a wonderful human being. When we told him we wanted to become his band, he said, "I didn't realize I needed a band because all these years I've been without one." But then he thought about it for a second. "Maybe this could work because sometimes when I go and play, you might be the only ones laughing." Then he asked us what we called ourselves. We had to finally admit we didn't have a name. I'll always remember his answer: "Well, what I'd like to call you, they couldn't print it." Then he said, "How about the Rascals?" We went with it, and it stuck.

When we weren't playing in clubs, we were practicing in the basement of my parent's house. It was directly across from Pelham High School, and we'd have all the basement windows wide open; the sound pouring out onto the street. It wasn't long before the kids began standing out on the sidewalk listening to the earliest days of what would become the Rascals. Pretty soon, it was a whole neighborhood scene, with teenagers out in front of Dr. Cavaliere's house dancing and singing along to our music. My sister, Fran, and Aunt Emma would be there cooking for all of us. Here you had the scent of Italian food wafting out the windows along with the rhythms of rock and roll. It was special.

Back then, as we blossomed into this neighborhood phenomenon, everybody supported us. There was even a neighborhood guy who made stickers with the band's name on them that he distributed to the kids on the street. Eventually, neighborhood people helped with our stage outfits, though not the schoolboy knickers that we wore during our earliest days of fame and fortune. Everybody pitched in because everybody felt like they had a stake in our success. We were like them. We were from the same place, and they wanted us to succeed. They believed in us, and we were beginning to believe in ourselves, too.

That belief paid off in the summer of 1965 when this gentleman came up to us in a club one night. Out of nowhere during one of our breaks he told us about a new venue he was opening in the Hamptons and that he wanted us to be the house band. The place, called The Barge—a floating night club in Westhampton Beach—was an actual barge. This, as they say, was our big break. Wealthy people flocked to the Hamptons like swallows to San Juan Capistrano, and it wasn't long before The Barge became the place throughout our summer in the Hamptons.

We signed on and waited for The Barge to open and in the meantime continued to play the Choo Choo Club. One evening, Eddie took off with our road manager and got into a terrible car accident. It was so bad that the driver died. The road manager was literally bandaged from his head to his feet. Eddie was asleep in the backseat and survived. I think that being out cold may have saved him, although he suffered a punctured lung, broken teeth, and God knows what it did to him mentally. That had to be tough. But this was just before we were supposed to go to work at the Barge, and the Rascals were about to never happen.

Eddie was, at that time, the front man of the band. He did a lot of singing, he was a great little dancer, and he was a great little showman. The girls all loved him. Now, he was injured. I didn't know what to do. I went to see Eddie's mother, and she was an angel from heaven. She was one of the sweetest women you'd ever want to know. She told me that Eddie had been really despondent since the accident. I looked her in the eye and said "Mrs. Brigati, this is very important. If we're ever going to make it, we're going to make it in this place because everybody who's anybody in the music industry, in the film industry, on Wall Street will be coming to this place.

"I promise you," I told this dear, sweet woman. "They've given us a home right across the street from the Barge, right on the beach. I'll watch Eddie like he's my brother. I promise you. We'll take him right home after the show every night. We'll watch him. We'll look after him. I'll make sure he goes right home to bed." She thought about it for a minute and said Eddie could do it if he wanted to and that we'd have her blessing. And with that, all four of us hit The Barge. It was idyllic, an amazing setting. The beach was there, the girls were there. The place was happening. The Rascals—name and all—were born.

I have found that those of us who lose a parent at an early age attempt to fill those profound voids left in the wake. I think that's what I was doing a lot of in those days. Ruby Toy, the woman who brought me into contact with Dino, was part of that. Things accelerated pretty quickly between us. She not only found me a new drummer, but she soon also became the mother of my first two children.

During the whole time as the Rascals were on the brink of taking off, I also had these two beautiful kids, first a son, then a daughter. The problem was that I wasn't ready to be a father. Ruby and I really weren't compatible, and we'd made a mistake. But I had obligations to live up to, making sure they had food and a place to live.

So, while we were trying to get to the big time, I was also trying to come to grips with what seemed like an almost untenable situation given the Catholic family I came from. I was on the brink of great success in the music business but also had two children and their mother to support.

These are the kinds of things that today seem almost ridiculous to think about, but, in those days, it wasn't so common. It was a big deal. My family really could not understand what made me tick. It wasn't clear to me, either.

In further filling the void, I found that forming The Rascals was to me like finding a brotherhood. I think I saw Eddie like the younger brother I never and I always wanted. That had a lot to do with how we clicked. It was like a big brother-little brother relationship. That's probably why it worked.

We were drawing huge crowds at The Barge. Celebrities like Bette Davis became regulars, as did many other musicians, like Al Kooper, who would later form Blood, Sweat, and Tears. We'd do our versions of hit songs, and it was nothing short of a love fest every night.

One such evening, as Gene remembers it, we'd just finished our set but were told we had three minutes left, so we played a song we'd been playing in New Jersey but hadn't yet brought to the Barge. It was about six or seven months later that "Good Lovin" became the #1 song in America. The Barge was such a great place to play, and for me, it's where I found three brothers with who I connected with both spiritually and musically. As Gene puts it, "We were like four people with one heart."

Adrian Barber became our sound man in and around the time we played The Barge. Adrian had been the sound man for the Beatles in Germany and had accompanied Joey Dee back to the U.S. With Adrian's expertise, those walking up the gangplank leading into the Barge were completely surrounded by sound. It was an incredible sensation, pretty much unheard of in those days.

It wasn't long before we began getting noticed by several different record labels. It began when Walter Hyman came into the club. Walter, a millionaire several times over who made his money in textiles, saw us, heard us, and immediately called his good friend Sid Bernstein. Sid was already considered a major player in the music business when he came out to the Barge at Walter's suggestion. Sid, a concert promoter, was about to bring the Beatles to the United States. The man had all the connections you would ever need in the music industry. The two—Walter Hyman and Sid Bernstein—offered us a contract, signing us right there on the spot. The impact was tremendous. One sit-down with the club's owners and our salaries were doubled.

In those days, you used the newspaper columns to publicize yourselves. Through Sid and Hyman, we began getting write-ups in the Daily News and the Post. One of the first people to want to produce our records was Phil Spector, an absolute legend who had originated what came to be called "the wall of sound," involving overdubbed vocals and instruments, leading to a signature and immediately recognizable sound.

The band was excited by Phil Spector's interest. However, I had a different vision of our sound. I felt it in my blood, and as hard as it was to say no, I told my bandmates that as much as I love Phil Spector's records, I didn't want us to sound like those records.

I wanted our sound, the sound we'd been capturing live. I had a clear vision of how we should present ourselves. Our sound was based on a Hammond organ, a funky guitarist, a dynamic drummer, and great singing. I didn't want anybody to tell us how to be or how to sound.

I held firm, feeling that just as important to signing a recording contract were the ensuing recordings themselves. This was the stance we took in turning down a handful of record contracts before Atlantic Records came a calling.

And here's where the grace of God once again comes in. It came in the form not only of Atlantic Records but in the person of a genius who "got" what we were about. His name was Arif Mardin, an A&R man at the time. A&R stands for artist and repertoire—the people who pick songs for the acts and help shape how they're recorded. He did it for hundreds of acts, most of whom you'd recognize.

What made Atlantic so great was that they approached their music the way jazz acts do. A jazz act plays and captures a moment of time in their recording. That's the difference between then and now. Here's an example of how they would make a record. First, you get John Coltrane and Miles Davis in a room, and then you put them in front of a microphone and let them play. That way, you capture the "liveness" of that performance. That's what we were after. And that's how Atlantic was used to doing things. It was a perfect match.

So, now I had a band, a name, and a recording contract with a record label I greatly respected and felt respected us as musicians. We made great music during those years at Atlantic, helped by some of the most talented people in the recording industry, allowing Eddie and me to write the songs for which we're known to this day. Along the way, we would meet, and some days record, alongside the greatest R&B artists of their day—people like Sam and Dave, Otis Redding, Wilson Pickett, and Aretha Franklin. We all had one thing in common: it was music, and there was plenty of it pouring out of the Atlantic Records building in downtown Manhattan.

I had no way of knowing then that my path with those four lads from Liverpool would again cross, first through our manager, Sid Bernstein, but also through the kind of music they were bringing to the U.S.—music that would influence and make us grow as musicians and songwriters, while testing the boundaries and, at times, patience, of Atlantic Records executives. All things seemed possible. With Atlantic strongly behind us, we knew that the next big super group was going to come from New York—and it was going to be us! But before that, there would be another name change and—oh, yeah, those schoolboy outfits that made us look like we just escaped from high school detention. But nothing could stand in our way. We had a record contract with a label I'd pretty much worshipped since I was a kid. I was about to meet many of my boyhood musical idols and, thanks to Atlantic, would even become colleagues with some of them.

Chapter 3: The Atlantic Years

◆

Motown Records' roster of amazing artists included Diana Ross, Smokey Robinson, Marvin Gay, Stevie Wonder, and The Temptations, just to name a few. Atlantic Records had Ray Charles, Otis Redding, John Coltrane, the Drifters, and Ben E. King, just to name a few. And while Barry Gordy didn't come knocking on our door, Ahmet Ertegun sure as hell did.

Ahmet Ertegun, the son of Turkey's first ambassador to the United States, had a maddening love affair with jazz and what was then called 'race music' until future Atlantic Records VP Jerry Wexler brilliantly coined the phrase 'rhythm & blues.'

I've always believed that it was Ahmet's love of jazz and his devotion to the great artists of the day that generated such a profound sense of music first. A handful of the great actors in Hollywood—Charlie Chaplin, Mary Pickford, and Douglas Fairbanks—tired of the extreme demands put upon them by the film studios of the day created their own studio calling it United Artists, which allowed them the autonomy to match their artistic desires to their professional abilities. Ahmet Ertegun and Atlantic Records was the recording industry's version of United Artists.

Aretha Franklin's story seems to describe exactly what Atlantic Records was all about in and around the time we joined them. Aretha's previous record company had attempted to record her in the mold of great jazz singers like Ella Fitzgerald and Sarah Vaughn, but when her contract was up, she chose Atlantic Records. Why? Because Atlantic and Aretha shared the same vision, which was to put Aretha back in church. In other words: let the queen of soul be the queen of soul.

Atlantic let us know right off the bat they were going to put us in the room with a couple of producers—Arif Mardin and Tom Dowd—they were going to be there solely to help us achieve our sound. In short, we were going into the recording studio with the goal of capturing our live sound. On top of that Atlantic provided us with free studio time which, to me, was incredible because it was unheard of at the time. Their call to arms was as simple as it was music to our ears: "Go on in there and do your thing until you're satisfied." Nobody does that.

The first time I stepped into the room, the very studio where so many of the records in my collection were made, I knew I was in a special place. It was as if the essence of my heroes were right there bouncing off the sound-inspired walls. It was special, yet beyond the history was the present. We were with a company that I truly believe wanted to make good music, where music was front and center, the reason why Atlantic existed.

Arif Mardin was a brilliant arranger, producer, and composer. As the story goes, Arif approached Quincy Jones while in his native country of Turkey and handed him a cassette of his work. I don't remember whether they were songs he wrote or arranged, but Quincy was so impressed that he got Arif a job teaching at Berkley, where among what would become a legendary list of credentials, he became a professor, shaping a whole generation of young musicians. While we were Arif's first big project, he'd go on to work with a dizzying list of artists, including Aretha Franklin, Roberta Flack, Bette Midler, Phil Collins, and in more recent years, Norah Jones. Having Arif around was like having the Encyclopedia Britannica of music sitting right there in front of you.

Making a record is like taking off your clothes in front of the world and then standing there and saying, "Hey, how do I look?" Good producers—and Arif was a Hall of Famer—make every song into a project. They also have to be extremely even-tempered. To give you an example, once Dino really didn't like the way a song was going, and Arif handled the situation without placating him or making him feel looked down upon. If one of us would say something foolish during the recording process, he'd deal with it in such an easy-going, matter-of-fact manner that he never seemed to piss anyone off. Because more often than not, if a producer ticks off the artist, that's it. He's gone. Arif could see things from the musician's point of view and keep the moment calm. That was a real gift.

Arif embraced the Atlantic philosophy of recording music. It went like this: when you play, it's like a time capsule. The goal is to make the music happen in the room, to capture that special moment. That philosophy came from Atlantic having its roots as a jazz label, and jazz is all about improvisation, right? No two performances are ever the same.

The Atlantic credo was to capture the artist in the moment instead of attempting to duplicate it again and again, no matter how many takes. For the Atlantic people, as well as for us, it must have sometimes seemed like a grand experiment, taking us, a group who were only used to playing live and putting them into a "laboratory" to create. We had to learn that process and, fortunately, in addition to Arif, we had another truly brilliant mind in Tom Dowd, the man who's pretty much credited with inventing multi-track recording.

Six months before we hit the studio, Atlantic sent Tom out to record some of our live shows at the Barge. It was a great move on their part. The goal, what we strived for, was to capture the magic of our live performances. We were all on the same page, which is as wonderful as it is rare. Tom's unique abilities and knowledge helped to lead the way, he had a great ear, and knew a hit when he heard it. Do you remember that song "Black is Black" from the '60s? Tom heard it done by some group from Spain and figured it would be a hit in the U.S., which it became by the group Los Lobos. That was Tom's insight.

Tom literally built his own gear, his own recording boards. That's how talented these people were. They created a lot of the things that became standards in the music industry, including the eight-track recording machine, that major advancement I've talked about, which was only in existence with Les Paul at Atlantic in those days. Nobody else had it. It's amazing. And Tom Dowd was a big part of that, a huge part.

I used to pick Tom's brain because he had recorded giants like Ray Charles and Ben E. King, which he would tell us about. There was one subject, however, that Tom never discussed. Most likely because it was top secret. It was the work he had performed on the Manhattan Project. I found that out years later at his memorial service and was blown away. He never said a word about it.

Tom was unbelievably brilliant, but when he tried to get into Columbia University to do some graduate work, they wouldn't let him in. That's a true story. He applied and they turned him down, saying he wasn't qualified. So, instead, he went into the music business. That shows you how funny God works. Here he had worked on an historic project, and he never said a word. He just quietly went into the music business and made more history with the technology he invented there, including the concept of stereo, which he mastered while at Atlantic.

The strides Tom made even prompted President Kennedy to fly him into Washington so that he could record his press conferences in stereo. Kennedy, going back to his fascination with the space program, was always on top of the latest technology, and stereo was one of the new toys at the time.

Stereo was great for the listener, but it actually gave us a lot of problems. First, it had to do with the way vinyl was pressed, the way they cut the grooves in the record. Bass required more grooves on the record's surface, and that meant it cut down on the number of minutes you could put on a side. It also affected the volume at which the record was reproduced. So, for instance, at a party, if someone put on a stack of records, the ones with the highest volume would be the ones people heard and paid attention to—the same was true on the radio. Bass, while it sounded good (we called it a "fat groove"), also cut down on the length and the volume of a song. So, the idea was to keep the groove low and the volume high. It was kind of a pain, creatively, to tell you the truth, but it's what had to be done.

Stereo meant every song had to be mixed twice into two versions: once in mono (one channel), and again, a second time, in stereo (two channels). The mono version was what DJs would play on AM radio stations. You had to have a mono version—one where all the sound on the record was recorded to come out of one speaker—because, otherwise, those listening on the radio would miss half that song. An example would be "Good Lovin'" The "1-2-3" before we started singing was right there on mono; in stereo, it danced back and forth between the left and right channels, but, if you didn't have a proper stereo setup, the "1-2-3" was lost.

For example, I was in a friend's house, and he had a good stereo system, but for some reason he kept the left speaker in the living room and the right speaker in the kitchen. I told him, "Do you have any idea how hard we worked to make this sound right, and you screwed up the whole thing." Nevertheless, as people started to have stereo systems in their homes, listening to popular music in stereo, as in left and right speaker separation, started to become more the standard.

For quite some time, smaller radio stations, especially in the southern part of the United States, still insisted on mono recordings because they didn't have the stereo needles required to get the full two-channel sound out of the stereo version of the record. Between the length (singles had to be shorter for radio airplay) and the stereo issue, the album versions of songs like "Lonely Too Long" are longer than the singles. That difference had a big impact on how songs were envisioned, produced, and heard when we were at Atlantic, but it wasn't only us, and it wasn't only at Atlantic; it was everybody.

When we recorded "Good Lovin'," I think we all knew we were on our way. I remember going into the recording booth where Tom Dowd was engineering the session and I said to him, "Tom, you know what, man? I think we can do that better"

He looked at me and put his hands around the recording console in a protective way. "You're going to have to go through me to do that again. I'm not letting you do it." That's where the expertise came in, where the professionalism came in because artists always think they can do it better. But he said, "This is it; this is magic. This is a smash hit." And he was right.

Atlantic was used to doing things the way jazz is done. It was a whole different thing from today. You had to play. Producers are the guys who are responsible for the final product. Producers were just starting to emerge on the recording scene, and most of them were very new at it, but we had the real deal in Arif. As Gene Cornish recalls from those days, the way you heard it on the record was the way we played it. No overdubs or enhancements. Just the way we played it. We loved that approach because it was the way we played in the clubs. But the new changes in recording also made so much more possible. Increasingly, there were sounds we could get in the studio that we could never have done live, on stage. We were enthralled by what we could achieve in the studio, and we lived there. We were able to create, unencumbered by financial considerations because, as I said, we weren't paying for the studio time. It's a big deal to me that they were willing to give a bunch of kids like us that opportunity. The way I describe it is Atlantic gave us this beautifully fertilized piece of land, and all we had to do was get this little seed, pop it up in the air, put it down in that earth, and it grew into this gorgeous, gorgeous plant.

In the beginning, after we got our record deal while at the Barge, we went in and recorded the songs Atlantic gave us. For the same reason we couldn't play our own songs in the clubs, we weren't encouraged to record them, either. The club scene and the record business shared a similar goal: familiarity, not creativity. So, we did "Land of a Thousand Dances" at the Barge in those days; we also did a lot of Smokey Robinson covers. Some of the songs I'd found that they would let us play were ones like "Good Lovin'," "Mustang Sally," and "In the Midnight Hour." It's kind of natural that those were the first songs we recorded on our debut Atlantic album in 1966.

There's no question we had good instincts about what songs worked and what songs didn't. When you work in front of people, when you have an audience, there's an instant reaction. You could feel it, and so could the record company. Atlantic could tell when something got that reaction. The first day we played "Good Lovin'" people got out of their seats and danced to it; they got up and sang.

It wasn't long before Atlantic recorded Wilson Picket's rendition of "Land of a Thousand Dances." He also had a hit with "Mustang Sally," which we first put on the "B" side of "Good Lovin'."

Because it was such a giant, number one record, a lot of people think that "Good Lovin'" was the first song we recorded at Atlantic, but, in fact, it was "I Ain't Gonna Eat Out My Heart Anymore," another song we didn't write. It was written by the team of Pam Sawyer and Lori Burton, who also wrote a ton of songs for Motown acts. Eddie did the lead vocal, and it was kind of a different song to the extent that he spoke, didn't really sing, the first lyrics. As they say, you have to start somewhere and the record, though it reached only #52 on the U.S. charts (it did better in Canada, reaching #23), performed well enough to get us on a popular TV show called "Hullabaloo" on February 27, 1965—our first television appearance.

That catapulted us to recognition. The fact that song got us on the TV show made Atlantic want to release our next single— "Good Lovin'," which made it to #1 that following spring of 1966. Atlantic suddenly wanted to put out an album of material—they were becoming the big thing in the 60's—but we still didn't have any of our own songs yet, so it was filled with covers like Bob Dylan's "Like a Rolling Stone," another

Sawyer-Burton tune titled "Baby Let's Wait," and "Mustang Sally," which, as I said, was the B side of "Good Lovin'" The only song we had anything to do with writing was "Do You Feel It," which, oddly enough, wasn't written by me and Eddie (as all of our future hits would be), but me and Gene.

There's nothing like the feeling of hearing your song on the radio. I mean, it's always a kick to hear yourself on the radio, but the first time is especially magical. All I can is, "WOW." There's nothing that can compare to that rush you get when you're in your car, in a store, anywhere there's a radio, and on comes your song. "Good Lovin'" coming out of those speakers and into the air where millions of people could hear it. It was magic. Hearing Cousin Brucie introduce, "Aint Gonna Eat out My Heart," and then "Good Lovin'" remains among my greatest thrills in life, the memories, Cousin Brucie's voice, so vivid.

"Cousin Brucie" Bruce Morrow is one of my longest lasting relationships in music and is someone who I truly consider family. Cousin Brucie has always been one of my biggest supporters and a great friend of the RASCALS. He controlled the airwaves on WABC FM, one of the most powerful radio stations on the East Coast, where he did over four-thousand broadcasts in thirteen years until 1974.

He was one of the biggest DJs in NYC and gave Murray The K a run for his money as NY's number one DJ in the mid '60s. Morrow was always an innovator and pioneer. His shows were a HIT with the teenagers. He would combine Pop, rock, soul, R&B and surf music. He was a fixture at teenage events and concerts throughout NY and New Jersey.

Cousin Brucie would go on to be partner with Robert Sillerman, creating the Sillerman-Morrow Radio Station Group. As far as I know he was the first radio talent that diversified and became an owner of radio stations. This legend's career has been in full bloom for more than six decades, most recently from 2005-2020, where he hosted oldies programming on Sirius XM before going back to WABC where it all began.

I have been so very fortunate to be on his radio shows and even perform for him on his live shows like Cousin Brucie's Palisades Park reunion concerts in NEW JERSEY. Still to this day he supports every show, my new music, and even this book. My manager said that he was going to write the forward to this book. So I am very excited, very humbled and very thankful. Thank You Cousin Brucie for the knocking on sixty years of friendship and the tremendous support you have always given me.

To this day, when I'm walking through a grocery store, and one of our records comes on in the background as people shop, I think to myself, *'Hey, these people don't know that's me!'* It's still a kick; all these years later, it never gets old. And it's all because we had such a great start at Atlantic.

The atmosphere that Atlantic created was out of this world. It was like being a painter and having every color available to you. We had all the musicians of a philharmonic available to us. If we wanted to bring in strings, we'd have the best in the world right there in New York City. We wanted to use French horns; they were there. We could color our music anyway we wanted. Whatever we wanted, it was there. Forget the candy store. I thought I'd died and gone to heaven.

The physical set-up of the Atlantic building, the way it was organized, had a lot to do with that. It was all right there in the same building on 59th Street. On the second floor were the studios; behind was the mastering area where the records were finished, and past the elevator were the secretaries and, after them, the higher-ups. So, when you made a record, the sound from the studio was heard for the first time by the secretaries. And then, if they liked it, they'd tell the higher-ups. Then the bosses would come in, and if they started dancing, it was magic!

Atlantic gave us the very best equipment there was, the state-of-the-art recording tools of the day. To give you some idea, we had eight tracks of recording for our records. That meant you could spread out the tracks. Lead vocals on its own track, background vocals on another, bass on its own track.... other companies had only four tracks to record on, so performers were very limited. The Beatles, the Stones, everybody, had just four tracks. Frank Sinatra, for example, recorded primarily on one track for all those classic records, and he was Sinatra! They just hung a microphone in front of him, recorded it, and that was it: instant mono recording. It sounds a little primitive, but that's how it worked at the time.

For us, having those extra tracks on which to capture sound was like a dream come true. If the performance was magical, and that's what I always wanted it to be, we had more ways to capture it. The additional tracks went a long way in making a lot of the songs you know from our records possible because we had both the techniques and the guidance available to achieve the exact sound we were looking for.

At that time, Atlantic was a small company, so they needed hits. It was the hits that kept them in the game. Those guys knew their music. So, when we were asked to be literally the first white act on Atlantic Records, I was thrilled. It was an amazing compliment. To be fully accurate, Atlantic did record white acts, just not on the Atlantic label. They had Atco—one of their other labels—for white artists like Bobby Darin and Sonny and Cher. Over the years, Atlantic brought on board groups like the Average White Band, interesting, considering how far they'd come from being pretty much an all-black label before we appeared.

Here we were—me, Eddie, Gene, and Dino—twenty-year-old kids working around so many of the performers whose records I'd bought: the Drifters, Clyde McPhatter, the Coasters—they were all there right there in Atlantic, hanging out in the halls and recording in studios. It was like my entire record collection coming alive in front of me! I was really proud to be there. Looking back now, over five decades later, it seems miraculous! Otis, Aretha, all the greats.

We became studio rats, practically living inside that room, twelve or fourteen hours at a time. I remember Wilson Pickett was overheard to say, "What's with those Rascals? They're always in that damned studio, and I can't get in there." We were making a lot of noise, that's for sure, and it attracted the attention of many others who recorded for Atlantic.

There's the story of Otis Redding, who stuck his head inside our recording room, and with wide eyes and an even wider smile, shouted, "My God, they are white!" I guess the great Otis Redding couldn't believe his ears when hearing the sound in the hall outside the studio. What Otis heard that day was the root of what I'd learned from all those records in the New Rochelle record store where I'd searched the bins and found the essential sound of the black artists who made up the core of the Rascals' sound.

Otis was a great pathfinder in our business. He was very aware of his rights and knew, like so few people did back then, that publishing and owning his own songs was the way to go. It was a great compliment that the great Otis Redding thought our music measured up to the great Atlantic artists of the day. Otis was certainly Atlantic's biggest star at the time, but it wouldn't be long before Aretha Franklin came over to the label. I knew of her time at Columbia Records and, of course, had heard all her records. I was thrilled when she came to Atlantic, even though she supplanted us as the number one act there at the time. The people at Atlantic treated her like royalty. They'd listen to her every whim.

She wasn't without her troubles, though. The man she was married to at the time would come to the studio for her sessions and sometimes get out of control, like yelling, making a scene and all that. But thankfully it didn't last long. When what we might call domestic situations get in the way of the music business's money-making machine, that kind of trouble disappears quickly—and this guy did disappear. He was shown the door and we never saw him again. Where he ended up is anybody's guess, but it certainly wasn't anywhere around Aretha.

The great thing about Atlantic, besides the music pouring out of that building, was the lack of barriers between us and the black artists who were pretty much the whole label, except for us. I'd always been in so-called "mixed" groups. Race never mattered to me, and I didn't get why other people got hung up on it. I will say, though, that I was pretty naïve about the role it played in the music business in terms of how black artists were paid in those days and, in some instances, weren't paid. It was at Atlantic that I got my first awakening to how the business had really screwed a lot of the older singers and songwriters out of the money they earned and deserved.

One day I was talking with Sam Moore, of Sam and Dave, who were on Atlantic at that time, and told him I really liked one of their songs, "Soul Man," I think it was, that I'd heard on the radio that same day. I figured I was giving him a compliment. Instead, he snapped back at me with, "Little brother, let me talk to you. We ain't making no money off of that. It's time to grow up, Felix." Like I said, it was an awakening and a pretty rude one at that. It was that day that I woke up to the idea that those guys were paid for the session, but they didn't get any royalties because they hadn't written the song, you see. It was a large club. Many of these guys were in the same boat. The great Jackie Wilson, as I recall, died without any health care whatsoever, despite having giant hits like "Lonely Teardrops" and "Higher and Higher." Too many of these guys died in poverty and that's a disgrace.

There's a story about Ray Charles, one of my earliest musical heroes. I heard from a number of musicians who were around Ray at the time about how club owners and others- would literally take advantage of his being blind and steal his money. Eventually, those who looked after him on the road would sew up the pockets in his jacket and pants to protect others from slipping money out—or drugs in. It's no wonder that so many black artists, to this day, insist upon getting paid before they go onstage. The business is full of stories about people who played and then were told to get lost without getting paid. It's one reason so many musicians walk around with cash on them or in the trunks of their cars. There was always this idea that if you didn't get paid, or you got robbed, at least you could get to the next town or sleep in a motel on the way. It was time to grow up, Felix. I'll always remember the day Sam told me that. It was a real education.

It also explained why guys like Wilson Picket, who I alluded to earlier, would have such a chip on their shoulder. They were big stars, making a lot of money for the label, but never really got their fair, full share. Sure, he had hits with "Mustang Sally" and "Midnight Hour," songs that Atlantic basically took, but that still didn't make him happy—or rich. I started to get a sense that, among us artists within the building and in the studio, Atlantic was a happy place to create, grow, and produce, but the business itself was not for the weak of heart or soul. Even at such a young age, I matured by seeing what my elders went through, and that was not a place where I wanted to end up.

For our part, during those great Atlantic days, we couldn't have had better guidance, both in and out of the studio. First, we really had people looking out for us. When we joined Atlantic, Sid Bernstein set us up with everything a twenty-something-year-old kid didn't know he needed, like a lawyer, a publishing company, a live performance company, a pension plan, retirement savings—you name it. We were our own corporation, and in return, we'd signed a management contract with Sid and his partner, Walter Hyman. Walter was really the "silent" partner in the relationship; he treated us cordially, but Sid really embraced us.

It was during these years that Sid took our band to his office and introduced us to Steve Weiss, a lawyer who represented both Sid and Walter. Steve was direct and to the point. "If you want, I'll represent you, too. I'll take five percent of your gross and take control of every part of your life!" Sounded like a good idea to us, though we weren't sure it was legal! Still, over time, Steve did the same deal for Jimi Hendrix, Led Zeppelin, and Peter Noone, among others. In the process, he became an extremely powerful man in the music business, especially in the Warner record group (of which Atlantic eventually became a part). Thanks to Sid, the business side of our lives was very well handled, leaving us free to create, which is exactly what we did!

Another pioneer of the recording industry was Jerry Wexler, co-owner and vice-president of Atlantic, credited with having coined the term "rhythm and blues." Jerry was the guy I mainly had to deal with. He was so fiery and would get so animated and heated in discussions that he even had a bottle of nitroglycerin on his desk just in case. He used to yell at me all the time when we'd fight over what singles to release, but he was a really, really good man.

Jerry had an interesting background. He started out as a music journalist before moving into the recording industry. His whole concept of making a record was based on something Berry Gordy did at Motown—mixing the songs so that they would sound good coming out of a little "box," which was essentially the way we listened to music in those days: on a small transistor radio, with a tiny speaker. The idea was that if it sounded good on that small radio, it would sound good anywhere. There was a sort of artistry to that approach, the ability to satisfy the ear with a song all the way down to the car speakers that weren't very good in the '50s and '60s, certainly not compared to today.

Not only were the three of these great men—Arif, Tom, and Jerry—unbelievably talented human beings, they were gentlemen who treated us like peers.

We were blessed to work with so many incredible musicians at Atlantic Records, people who were truly artists in their own right, people like Chuck Rainey, a fantastic bass player who played on just about every Rascals record made in those Atlantic days, including the bass line on

"How Can I Be Sure." Ron Carter, another bass player who, to this day, is an extraordinary jazz musician, played on our records. It was really a stroke of great luck to have these guys because no band had bass players like these. People don't necessarily know that while Eddie, Gene, Dino, and I were the core of the Rascals, we had others who regularly contributed to the records you heard. Eddie's brother, David, who I met in the "Starliter" days, sang background vocal on a lot of our records. King Curtis, one of the finest sax players of his time, probably of any time, also played on some of our sessions. That was a really big deal because here was somone who played with artists as diverse as Buddy Holly, Cannonball Adderly, Waylon Jennings, and Andy Williams. As a session player, he played on records by Aretha Franklin and the Coasters. With his own band, he and Jerry Wexler put together a number of hits, including "Soul Twist," and he even opened for the Beatles at their 1965 Shea Stadium concert.

Do you remember the cover of our first album? It was called "The Young Rascals." That was very interesting because we had come to Atlantic as "The Rascals," the name Soupy Sales had bestowed upon us, but now we were "Young Rascals." There was a lot of show business stuff going on behind the scenes around this time that I didn't exactly like but had to live with. Our manager, Sid Bernstein, had a vision for what people wanted, and that vision HELPED GET us to Atlantic, but the recognition we were getting, ironically, also led to forcing us to change our name. It wasn't Sid's choice, but he was worried about a phone call he received from the manager of this group called "The Harmonica Rascals." They were really big at the time, regulars on the "Milton Berle Show" on TV. One day Sid called and said, "You're going to have to change your name, or you're going to get sued." So, to avoid that whole legal mess, we became "The Young Rascals" overnight. I thought it was stupid at the time and never really liked the name, but I guess, in retrospect, I can see the necessity.

Of course, the name "Rascals," young or not, presented another series of problems, related to the TV show "The Little Rascals," which featured a bunch of kids who were always getting into trouble. It also was a big hit, and, for a very long time, people confused our name with theirs. To this day, there are some people who still don't get the difference between our name and theirs. In fact, as an aside, when I was living in Connecticut back in the 1980s, I'd have people come up to me and ask if I still had the little dog (he was part of the Little Rascals TV show) that had a circle around one eye. They would ask if the circle was real or if it was painted on. After "Good Lovin'" and before our next hit record, we were able to shed the "young" and go back to being just the Rascals. It's something I insisted upon, though I think the other guys were pretty much on board with it, too.

While it lasted, it was a wonderful, wonderful time. Here we were—these four kids who, in six months, had gone from my parent's basement in Pelham to the heights of the record business at a label I had admired and respected since my first foray into rock and roll. Here we were in charge of our own destiny.

Being at Atlantic in those early days of the Rascals was like being part of a family, both in and away from the studio. I used to go to Arif's home, and we'd sit around and chart out and talk about arrangements of songs, and it was such a joyous occasion. Great songs become like your own creations being born and, with Arif and Tom nearby, we had the best doctors there in the room helping us with their birth. Both are gone now, Tom in 2002 and Arif in 2012, but the songs we recorded back then are as much a part of their legacy as they are of ours.

As our artistry grew during the Atlantic years, so, too, did what we wanted to say through our own music and lyrics. They increasingly became a reflection of our identity as a band and of who I was as a songwriter. They were a reflection of their day but have also withstood the test of time, and there's a story behind each of them. Some I've told before, but many, I think, might surprise you.

Chapter 4: Writing the Songs

Among my favorite things in life are the stories people, perfect strangers, and fans tell me. They share about how they had their first date at one of our concerts, how the first time they ever made love was to one of our songs, or how a song of ours helped them through a down time. Their stories never cease to both honor and humble me.

There was a man I met once who wanted to give me his dog tags from the Army. I asked him why. "You saved my life in Vietnam. I was on a boat," he continued. "Our job was to pick up the wounded on the May Cong Delta and I heard you guys were going to be on the television show Hullabaloo, and I didn't want to miss it, so I said I'll take the next boat. If I'd taken that first boat, I'd be dead because that boat went down, and everybody died."

Now, while all of our songs surely didn't save lives, I'd like to feel that a number of them may have changed lives.

When we started at Atlantic, we had everything we could possibly want except for one thing: our own songs, ones that we wrote ourselves. We had it good, but four guys from England were turning the rules of songwriting upside down. The Beatles quite simply re-wrote the rules and forever changed the way the recording business worked. Before they came along, it was unheard of for artists like Perry Como or Tony Bennett—even Frank Sinatra—to write their own music. They never wrote their own songs. The process was simple, maybe not creative, but certainly uncomplicated for recording artists.

Many amazing and talented composers—take Cole Porter for instance—would pen the songs, and the performers would go into the studio to sing and record them. So, this was a whole new development for us, the Rascals, and really for everybody in the music business. It was a revelation to all of us. No one had ever done this before. All of a sudden, it was about our credibility as artists. If we were going to be a legitimate band, a legitimate group, we had to have a legitimate stake in the creative side, which was the writing process.

I think I always knew that I wanted to be not just a musician but a songwriter and producer. Eddie was a great singer, but writing songs…? He needed a little convincing as it was unchartered territory. Writing, actually composing music, has always been where it's at. What's it like when you write a song? All I know is that, for me, it's more often than not an emotional experience. Going back to my parents' living room in Pelham, I'd put my hands on that keyboard, and I'd enter another dimension. I remember my dad, who never really understood my creativity, would sometimes come into the room. He'd clear his throat, maybe say something, and it would break the spell. He'd come up behind me and boot me out of my trance. Strange as it is, to this day, I can't stand having anyone behind me when I play.

Our process was less fluid than it was regimented. I'd write the music, I'd write the title, and most of the time, I'd write the chorus, as in "Beautiful Morning." It started with "It's a Beautiful Morning. I think I'll go outside for a while. And just smile." I'd create the template, and Eddie would fill in the verses. Eddie's main skill in songwriting was his ability to tell a story. He was an excellent lyricist. That's how it went, and we shared everything. Eddie was like the little brother I never had, and that came out in those early days when we collaborated on those songs. It was a pretty cool process and a great partnership.

Once Eddie and I would complete the initial writing portion of the song, I'd go over the music with Arif. Among Arif's many great abilities was in his seeing the forest through the trees. Taking in our song that we've become so engrossed within and helping us take a step back. That was our process. It was a great formula, and if we got stuck, we knew we could count on Arif, who always seemed so adept at handling whatever we threw at him.

It was the natural next step for us to write our own music and lyrics, but it was also a major risk because no one knows what's going to happen when you write a song and especially when you're following up on such a major hit, a monster of a song like "Good Lovin'." They call it the "sophomore jinx." Where would we go from there? The first song we wrote was "You Better Run." Expectations were high, and we had a rough time. I figured we'd write what we knew from the clubs, the songs that would get people up and dancing. "Come on Up" was that kind of song, one I wrote myself back in the Barge days. So, we had that one song, and Atlantic released it in 1967. It was a great club song, but it didn't get near "Good Lovin'" in terms of chart success.

"You Better Run" came out of a bad relationship I was in at the time. It was a very, very tense, difficult time in my life. It was about a person I was in a relationship with and probably shouldn't have been, which really isn't very unusual. Everybody has a relationship like that; everybody goes through that at some time in their lives. That was manifested in the song. It was kind of hard rocking. It was pointed, with a harsh sound. You can hear it in the lyrics. "Whatcha tryin' to do to my heart? Whatcha tryin' to do to my soul?" Like I said, it was a bad time in my life, and the song reflected that. Once I got past that time, the writing got happier because I was in a better place with a different lady. One good thing about "You Better Run" is that many years later, Pat Benatar recorded it and had a hit. Every time that happens—when someone covers your song—it brings more attention to your other music and, of course, increased royalties.

It was towards the end of this dark period where I recall working on a crossword puzzle and the word "muse" came up and the answer was "Erato." She was one of the seven muses in Greek mythology and provided the inspiration for a poet back in the second century. I remember leaning back and fantasizing about the powers of the muse.

It seems as if it was merely a matter of days before Adrienne Buccheri entered my life. She was beautiful, both inside and out, and I fell madly in love. There is no doubt in my mind, I truly believe she came into my life at that time to inspire me to write this music. The power of fantasy. The power of the muse.

All of a sudden, these wonderful love songs started to just pour out. What was even better was people really related to these songs. Along came "Lonely Too Long," and we got into the top 20. Thank goodness, because if that one song hadn't clicked, I'm not sure we would have been able to continue writing our own songs. The record company liked us, but they were in it to make money. That song came along just at the right time, and without it, I don't know that the Rascals would have gotten to where we did or that I'd be where I am now. That's why it still has a special place in my heart.

Another example is "How Can I Be Sure?" It also came out of the relationship with Adrienne. It was as if I began finding a pragmatist's sense of reality. Wondering whether this beautiful young lady was "the one" I'd be with the rest of my life. When I first played that for Arif, he immediately felt the French-sounding mode I'd put down. He wrote the string line against what we arranged. It was an ascending string line with the strings going up at one point in the song and then offset with a counter line that goes down. Invaluable!

Every time I play that song, I think of Arif, every single time, and I've played it thousands of times. He mentioned that to me years later. I remember he said, "Felix, you remember that French horn line I put in there?" And that's the thing. It's the joie de vivre you get when you make music, when you make a song happen. I truly believe that everybody at

Atlantic Records was about that in those days—even those on the business side. I can easily say that in terms of my years at Atlantic, I'm most proud of all those great songs that we wrote.

There really is no separating our songs from the instruments we used to write and record them. My vision was always to have the group's sound be based around the organ instead of being guitar-driven, which had an impact on how we wrote the songs. Although I composed the music on piano. Still, the foundation was the Hammond organ and everything—voices and instruments—would revolve around that. Part of it was hearing guys like Jimmy Smith, who mastered the organ and just blew me away the first time I heard him. I recall hearing a band back in the Pelham days, I believe they were called 'The Mighty Cravers.' The keyboardist was absolutely killing it, playing bass, playing rhythm, everything, all of it right there at his fingertips. It sounded as if he had an entire orchestra in one instrument and it was among the coolest sounds I'd ever heard. It was that sound that I wanted to one day build a band around.

With Eddie on vocals, Gene on guitar, and Dino on drums, there were so few limitations to the music we could write. Rhythmically we were very strong, and vocally we were very secure. Plus, thanks to Arif, we would introduce other instruments—French horns on songs like "How Can I Be Sure?" and a harp on "A Girl Like You." There was also the Beatles' influence as time went on because we began to hear things they did on the Sgt. Pepper album and began to explore songwriting that was more complex than the basic rock and roll structure.

Once again, I have to thank the Beatles for expanding our horizons in terms of songwriting. The radio stations in the '60s were the lifeblood of pop music. You could make a great record, but if the stations didn't want to play it, so what? Well, when the Beatles made a record, they had to play it. They had no choice. It was the Beatles, so even if the record was different or strange, the stations would play it. That really opened the door for us. "Michelle" and "Yesterday"—those weren't exactly rocking songs. They used different instruments, borrowed a lot from other musical genres, and made it basically "okay" to expand the range of what radio stations would play. It opened the door for Eddie and me to write songs like "How Can I Be Sure?" and add swinging brass to songs like "A Girl Like You," knowing the songs would be acceptable on top 40 radio. If the Beatles could do it maybe we could, too. It really kind of emboldened us to try new things in our songwriting, with the encouragement and expertise of Arif and Tom at Atlantic.

"A Beautiful Morning" in 1968 was born during one of the once or twice a year trips we used to take to Hawaii, where we would both play and relax. We became like the Beatles in Hawaii. For some reason, the Beatles really didn't capture the hearts and minds of Hawaiians like they did their fans on the mainland. Part of our popularity there no doubt came from a really big disc jockey named "The Beard," who loved rhythm and blues music. For reasons having to do with racial divisions in Hawaii at the time, he couldn't play R&B music on the radio. We were the closest thing to that kind of music he could play on the air, and so he just kept playing us and playing us and playing us and all of a sudden, we became very popular.

With all of that popularity and the beautiful weather, my theory became "The heck with the rest of the world; let's just stay here in paradise and be stars." Hawaii was a very important part of our story. We were like family to Hawaiians. In fact, they used the word "Ohana," which means family in Hawaiian, to describe us. We were coming off a number one record, I was madly in love, and the sun was shining, and it was so beautiful that I couldn't help but write a song to capture the moment dancing in my heart. I wanted every person who would ever hear this song to feel what I was feeling at that moment. I wanted everyone to feel that joy, that ecstasy I was feeling.

"A Girl Like You" was still about being in love, but I wanted to capture the feeling with horns. And again, Arif was instrumental with this as well. We'd sit down at his piano, and we'd go back and forth, and over the next few days, he'd come to the studio with the musical charts. He'd take my ideas and layer on his, and it was just magic. It was an unbelievably great experience.

"Groovin'," which sat at #1 for five straight weeks probably wouldn't even have been released if it hadn't been for the highly influential disc jockey Murray the K. It certainly wouldn't have been the "A" side of the record. Atlantic really didn't like the song very much because it had no drums on it. Murray came into the studio just to say hi on the same day we cut the record. He heard the playback of the song and instantly thought it was a hit. When he later heard that Atlantic didn't want to release it, he personally went to see Jerry Wexler and said something along the lines of "Are you crazy? This is a friggin' #1 record." Murray was right. "Groovin'" was #1 on the charts for five straight weeks, proving that once again, even the smartest record executives can be wrong.

Like Cousin Brucie, Murray the K was one of the original influencers of the Rock N Roll genre. He and Cousin Brucie, along with Alan Freed, were the most prominent DJs in New York City in the '60s. Some considered Murray the K the original hysterical disk jockey, and others the fifth Beatle as he was one of the earliest, most prominent DJs to get behind their music in the US. Simply put, Murray the K was a star, the man, and in New York, he was bigger than most of the acts whose records he spun. He was a true innovator who wouldn't just play the singles, he'd play some of the deeper album tracks and took great thrill in introducing unknown bands whose music he liked.

Needless to say that hearing The Rascals on the radio in those early days was an exciting time for all of us and our families, but the truest, most significant moments came in hearing the words that Murray the K and Cousin Brucie spoke when playing our songs. Two giants who I'd been listening to since I was thirteen were suddenly talking about me and my music. What a thrill! I'll forever treasure those memories as some of the greatest in my life.

The inspiration for "Groovin'" came about as a result of how and, more importantly, when we work as musicians, we mainly work at night, especially on Fridays and Saturdays when others are out enjoying themselves. And our girlfriends and wives are staying home while we're out working. And while we're definitely enjoying the hell out of it, they're home. So often the only time I really had free to be with my lady was Sunday afternoon. "Groovin" on a Sunday afternoon became like a Valentine's card to all those we left at home while we worked. I think people really related to that because a lot of people work evenings, a lot of people work weekends, and holidays and often times Sunday is that one day to be with their loved one. When I was growing up, stores weren't open on Sundays, the whole world seemed to go slower, you could hang out, enjoy that one day. It almost had a Sabbath kind of feeling. Now, of course, it's just like another day of the week. Back then, it was almost pastoral.

That song had a special feel, especially to the Latin community. It was one of the first songs ever done by a rock and roll group that had conga drums instead of regular drums. But at Atlantic, they were telling us things like "Latin? Latin? We don't do Latin." They just didn't want to put it out. It probably would still be in a vault somewhere to this day, never released, if Murray the K hadn't lobbied Jerry Wexler with the promise of guaranteed airplay on his radio show. It all goes to show that some of this is subjective. It's what some people hear that other people can't and maybe never will. I heard once that a record executive turned down the Beatles for a recording contract because he said their music had too much guitar and "guitar music was over."

"People Got to Be Free," was another record I had to fight Atlantic to release. This time they thought it was less about the music and more about the message. They didn't want the controversy they thought would come with the song. They insisted on staying away from what they thought of as politics, something they figured would turn off the audience. I argued that there was nothing controversial about freedom. How could freedom be controversial? Still, it was a battle. "People Gotta Be Free" came about when Bobby Kennedy was assassinated. I was on vacation and heard about it on a shortwave radio. That same day I got a phone call from a girl I knew who was in Los Angeles at the Ambassador Hotel right at the moment when RFK was shot.

I remember thinking about how right then and there the world might have changed. It was kind of a turning point in our writing. It was a very pure song, straight from the heart. That song, in my mind, had to be released. I knew that if we were going to survive as songwriters, as artists, sometimes we were going to have to fight for our beliefs. I'm glad we fought for "People Got to Be Free" and I'm very, very proud of that song. Bruce Springsteen once called it the definitive song of its time. He said he always felt that song in his heart. A lot of others must have felt it, too. It became #1 in many of the most oppressed parts of the world: the Union of South Africa, Hong Kong, China, and Berlin, before the wall had been torn down. It's something I'm very proud of because people got the message. To this day, when I play it in concert, I dedicate it to our troops around the world and always say that I'm going to keep playing it until they all come back home.

"Ray of Hope," which became a moderately successful single, was really my statement on the aftermath of RFK's assassination and the hope that his brother, Ted Kennedy, who I truly believed in, would carry on the torch of peace and justice. It was the first time I sang falsetto on the vocal. I think of it as my tribute to Curtis Mayfield, his solo work and his recordings with the Impressions being such an inspiration.

About 20 years ago, at a song writer's seminar held at the Bottom Line in New York, a gentleman named Mack Rice walked up to me and literally gave me a kiss, a big kiss smack on the mouth. He said, "You don't know it, but you saved my life." I couldn't wait to hear his story. "I was really in desperate straits," he said. "Then you put my song on the back side of "Good Lovin'." And then immediately after that, Wilson Picket recorded the song, and it became a hit. Putting that song on your record saved my life." "Mustang Salley" began playing worldwide ever since. It was used in movies and commercials and according to Mack Rice, the new life we gave the song completely changed his life. We evidently didn't know back then that the B-side of a 45 sells the same number of records as the A-side, and its writer makes just as much money when the record is a hit. It was a good learning experience, as well as a good deed for our karma!

For the most part, however, we never saw the flip side of a 45 as inferior to the supposed "hit" side. "B" sides were sometimes the songs that we played to please our peers. Songs that we loved or felt proud of that weren't seen by the record company as being "radio-friendly." The record executives didn't see them as commercially viable, even if the fans thought otherwise. Even today, I play some of them because they really took off with the fans. One is "Love is a Beautiful Thing," the B-side of "You Better Run." That's a song that was literally written in the studio. It was performed exactly as it was created, a totally spontaneous flow of creativity. As an aside, when I hear it, I'm reminded, for that reason and many others, of how great it is when you're part of a group—the creative energy that comes with that.

"What is the Reason?" is another "B" side, this one on the flip of "Come on Up" in 1966, that really resonated with people. Here's where that came from. I had real admiration for Phil Spector, the legendary producer who was also working at Atlantic at the time. I based that song on his kind of arrangement. I tried to emulate the bigness, the largeness of his sound on records he did with groups like the Ronettes and so many others he produced over the years. It came to be known as the "Wall of Sound" and used a lot of drums and bells. That's what I was trying for. Phil Spector, coincidentally, didn't like stereo. He was really a mono guy and thought everything sounded better coming out of a single, small speaker, so, like Motown, created this "big" sound for a "small" space. Today it's amazing how many true fans of early rock and roll want to hear the original mono versions of classic songs. Maybe Phil was on to something.

As we continued to write our own songs for the Rascals, we had to face a new reality. Singles weren't all the record companies wanted anymore because groups, starting with the Beatles, were now making "theme" albums. In many ways, it was a change that really excited me because I always felt like albums should be a little bit like complete operas, starting with a story and carrying that "theme" through from start to finish. Our initial album really pretty much capitalized on the singles we made and reflected what was going on with albums at the time: including one or two songs people knew from the radio and a lot of others that we loved performing on stage. The songs might have been good, but they weren't "connected" by a common theme. Nobody really knew what Sgt. Pepper was about, but it was by the Beatles and had enormous instrumentation, unbelievable production, and a sense that by the end it added up to a statement.

The Beatles forced us into thinking more seriously about the songs we wrote, not as individual songs but as part of an overall vision. After "The Young Rascals" and "Collections" came "Groovin'" and then what I call our concept albums: "Freedom Suite" and "Once Upon a Dream." When I look back on it, "Freedom Suite," especially, opened up so many doors. "Freedom Suite" reminds me that it's impossible to overestimate the influence of "Sgt. Pepper." Because of it, we started to take a sort of thematic approach to our work. It was similar, in some ways, to my classical music training as a child, especially in terms of the classical world of operas, which, as I said, are very thematic. I saw the Rascals getting into an area that would spin off into something more epic. The record company, on the other hand, was not very interested. To put it honestly, they could have cared less. Fortunately, however, that album produced the two hits, "People Got to Be Free" and the other "Ray of Hope." "Once Upon a Dream," which a half-century later would become the title of our Broadway show and tour, was an album on which we really stretched. From a musical perspective, it definitely was not what you would call commercial. I employed a twelve-tone structure in some of those songs and, at times, it actually sounded pretty dissonant. Arif was busy at the time, and we ended up with a different arranger, which didn't really help. That album became like our story book.

Story number one was the formation of the group, and story number two was how we progressed to an almost God-like level with our music. That became the most important thing to me—to reach a level of spirituality with our songs. To make and leave an indelible mark became increasingly and incredibly important. Our die-hard fans had been right there with us, but by changing formats and departing from our formula of hit singles, we pretty much lost a whole lot of others.

Our biggest selling album was a greatest hits compilation titled "Time Peace" in 1968. It was around that time that we were putting out two albums a year, which was a lot of songwriting output. Frankly, it's what really started to burn out Eddie. We were writing, then recording, and touring; then, we'd record some more and tour some more.

It was exhausting. We were out in San Diego around that time, and I wasn't feeling well and decided to go to Mexico, along with our road manager, Andy Leo. Some of it was because I wasn't feeling well. A lot of it was a kind of a protest.

We were paying a lot of taxes based on what we were earning, which was really a lot of money. I was very anti-war and didn't want all my money being spent on bombs. So, it seemed like a cool thing to just take off to Mexico as a protest of the Vietnam War. So I went there with our road manager, stayed for about a month, and got into a lot of crazy stuff, most of which remains a fog. In my absence, Sid Bernstein, bless his soul, was really getting nervous. "What are we going to do without Felix? When is he coming back?" These were the worries going on back at Atlantic. The other Rascals picked that time to have a sort of "mutiny." They convinced Atlantic that they could do a Rascals album without Felix. They wrote, recorded, and produced some new songs that, to this day, no one has ever heard because that album has never been released. It probably never will be. I've never even heard it.

Atlantic really wanted another album to keep the money train of the Rascals rolling. So, instead of waiting for my return from Mexico, they compiled our past work, mostly hit singles, into "Time Peace."

It fell on me for several years to run the band's business. I didn't always know what I was doing, but I did know each and every one of us had a talent. You had to satisfy everybody, both their ego and their talent. Dino, being the talented artist he is, became the art department, creating the design for the album covers. It was great because Dino was so good at it, a terrific visual artist.

When it came to writing songs, Gene gave us a little bit of trouble because he really wanted to contribute, but with the exception of one or two songs—I think he had "I'm So Happy Now"— his songs really didn't connect with people. It's difficult because having an equal voice in songs can be important to maintaining relationships within a group. Still, at this point, things were mostly amicable among all of us. It was all for one, one for all. It wasn't about the money. I always joke that we were like a bunch of socialists, sharing the wealth. We made mistakes, but never with the music.

That's not to say there weren't problems. For instance, Eddie really, I stress really, didn't like being in the studio in those days. He was young and just wanted to go around with girls and was having trouble keeping up with the song writing output. He would lean on his brother, David, I learned from others years later, when he was in trouble with the lyrics. This all became part of the growing tension within the Rascals. Still, we had to go out on the road, with our concert schedule predicated by every new record release. Sometimes we'd play new songs for the very first time while on the road, kind of try them out for the audience. There was so much excitement in that. I call it a kind of "dangerous fun."

The travel was intense. Performing before crowds so rewarding, meeting so many amazing people along the way, getting into scrapes we thought we might not get out of, and witnessing the innerworkings of our country from coast to coast and all avenues in between during the brilliant and turbulent '60s gave me and my brothers a magnified firsthand look at one of the most historic times in our nation's history.

Chapter 5: Adventures and Misadventures

I think a big part of my destiny started right in that record shop in New Rochelle. The bus I rode there was sort of like my path. It's the only way I can explain what guided me to the record bins in that store, filled with hidden gems by black artists who had never been exposed to white audiences, who had never had airplay on the major radio stations in New York.

It was that one piece of vinyl I found deep in the record bin. "Good Lovin'" made it possible to appear on television shows and play the biggest clubs and concert halls in America. The 45 was recorded by an R&B group called the Olympics and has since been recorded by dozens of other artists, from the Grateful Dead to Bobby McFerrin.

Today, the Rock and Roll Hall of Fame lists it among a select group—the 500 songs that shaped rock and roll—and it's also been called one of the greatest singles ever made. Not only that, it's on Rolling Stone's "Greatest Songs of All Time" list. I'm really proud of that. It made so much else possible that may not have happened otherwise. Then again, I always say I don't really believe in coincidence or chance. Destiny? That's something different, and I've always believed that, for some reason that I may never know, I was chosen to do what I do and bring the joy of music to others.

So much of our destiny—the Rascals' destiny—was really linked to the times and the groups around us. When the Rascals rode the charts with "Good Lovin'" in 1966, the Beatles were everywhere. They owned the airwaves and dominated record sales. Along we came—the Rascals—and it was like we were America's sweethearts, the answer to the British invasion; at least that's what my current manager says, and he may be right. So much of our destiny was tied in with the Beatles and others who were huge at the time with so much of our success tied to our touring the country, playing in such luminary landmarks as Madison Square Garden, Shea Stadium, and the Filmore West. And being invited to appear on the quintessential variety shows at the time, such as: "Ed Sullivan," "Mike Douglas," and "Hullabaloo."

We swept the country as "Good Lovin'" began its rise on the charts. The song was getting play, but we needed to hit the road, mainly hit the radio stations nationwide in promotion of either getting the song onto their top 40 rotation or, more often than not, helping to keep it there. We hit Connecticut, Massachusetts, NY, Philly, Baltimore… up and down the Eastern seaboard before heading west, to, as they say, connect the coasts.

You play, and you travel, and you play, and you travel, it's a dizzying venture of endless days. That doesn't mean there aren't memories, because there are, but when you're young and in the middle of all this success, it sometimes becomes a blur. All I can say for sure is we played a lot of places, were on a lot of top TV shows, and met a lot of interesting people along the way. I mean a lot of people, from other musicians to comedians, athletes, and politicians. Some were kind. Others, not so much. I only want to talk about those who were, because they helped the Rascals get to the top, and I remain ever grateful to every single soul who helped guide us on our path.

When I decided I wanted to be a musician, it didn't exactly excite my family. Let's go further and say my father, especially after my mother passed, really had reservations. For one thing, a lot of bands, back then, played in strip clubs. My father, a very strait-laced gentleman, was worried that being a musician meant that his son was going to play in those kinds of places. To put it directly, he had more than a casual fear about who his son was going to be associating with. The kind of people who ran those places, let alone the kind of people who went to those places, gave him a lot of reasons to worry. At least that's what he thought, and he probably wasn't wrong--not so much about where we would be playing, but about the music business itself and the people who ran it.

Fortunately, we mostly played in class venues, a lot of that had to do with our start in the Hamptons. We got used to being around what you might call, "polite society." Because of our playing at the Barge, we started to get noticed in the Hamptons and invited to a lot of the parties held by the affluent people who lived there. It was kind of a weird scene. Remember, we were kids in a place where there were a lot of rich and influential people. Sometimes it was hard to know how to act. Eddie, for example, nearly cleared the whole place at one party on a particular evening. Everybody there was talking about books and movies. Eddie said, in front of the host and a crowd of people, "What kind of party is this?" Far as I can tell, he was implying that parties weren't about talking, but having fun, especially with the young ladies for which he was always scanning the room. Eddie was like a buzz saw coming into a room, everybody loved him, he was that kind of guy, funny as hell, and endlessly engaging. He could get away with stuff that the rest of us probably couldn't. He was the clown. I was the serious one. We were a good match.

Maybe because of that, Eddie and I really started to pair off, just as Gene and Dino did to some extent. It could have been because of our songwriting roles, or possibly just because, in some weird way, we were more compatible at that time. We even had an apartment in New York for about a year, between 1968 and 1969, and I have to tell you, with Eddie around, that apartment sometimes seemed like a toll booth, with all the girls coming through. Despite those "distractions," we were still able to get work done, at least some of the time. Most of that work took us away from the studios at Atlantic and into America's homes and concert venues.

Just to give you some idea, in 1965, within a period of only four months, from August to November, we signed with Sid Bernstein, had a close brush with the Beatles at Shea Stadium (August), recorded our first single, "I Ain't Gonna Eat Out My Heart Anymore" (September), took up residency at the Phone Booth in Manhattan (October), while still continuing to play shows on an almost nightly basis. Then we filmed our first TV show (December). It was a whirlwind with no rest for the weary.

Our television debut, as I recall, was a show called "Hullabaloo" on NBC toward the end of December 1965. What made it stand out were the "go-go dancers" dancing in a kind of "cage" on platforms up above you. We did two songs, "I Ain't Gonna Eat Out My Heart Anymore," and "Good Lovin.'" We didn't really sing and play them live, but "mimed" or lip- synched them. That's how it went; the filming was staged for show, not sound. I'm not sure it fully registered with me at the time, but "Hullabaloo" had everybody who was anybody on it: James Brown, Jackie Wilson, Dionne Warwick, the Rolling Stones, the Supremes, Roy Orbison, the Animals, just to name a few. It was pretty cool to be in that kind of company. We appeared again on "Hullabaloo" the following February, in 1966, performing "Slow Down" as well as "Good Lovin'."

Some say the shows "Hullabaloo" and "Shindig" had a major impact on what has been termed "blue-eyed soul." Some writers point to acts like the Righteous Brothers, who pretty much grew their career on "Shindig" and Mitch Ryder and the Detroit Wheels, as helping to move blue-eyed soul forward. All I know is that the label "blue-eyed soul" began to be applied to us after Otis Redding first heard us recording at Atlantic—when he couldn't believe that soulful sound was coming from a bunch of white kids.

We were becoming big enough that Sid Bernstein got us an invitation to the Beatles concert at Shea Stadium in August of 1965. I think he saw it, no doubt, as free publicity, especially if he could get us noticed before the Beatles took the field. So, we were all there—me, Eddie, Gene, and Dino—in the Mets dugout, watching and listening to the opening acts and waiting for the Beatles. It was historic, in more ways than one. Sid somehow got the words "The Rascals Are Here" in huge letters posted up on the big scoreboard. It must have seemed like a good idea at the time, but not to Brian Epstein, the Beatles' manager. The man hit the roof. As the story goes, and I can't personally say I witnessed it, Epstein went to Sid and said something like "If that stays there" (pointing to our name on the scoreboard), the Beatles won't. The scoreboard, I'm told, went blank.

My memories of that night are of 50,000 screaming kids—most of them girls. The roar from the crowd when the Beatles first appeared, running across the ball field to the stage, was like a giant hysteria. In 1965, it was the first rock concert that had ever been held in a ballpark and those in attendance were only there for one reason and it wasn't to see us. But, let me add that we would be back, playing there ourselves in 1971. It's really something playing for that kind of crowd in a stadium. It was hard to hear yourself sometimes, especially back in the days before we had the technology we have today.

The Beatles made The Ed Sullivan Show on Sunday nights the place for teenagers to be. People always ask me about what it was like for us to perform on Ed Sullivan, probably because he had the one show that everybody wanted to be on. It wasn't just teenagers who tuned in on

Sunday nights, but entire families, all across America. Every week they'd feature at least one "pop" group to pull in the younger generation. We appeared a number of times, the first in March of 1966, doing "Good Lovin'." We were back again the following year, doing "Groovin'" and "A Girl Like You," and then, in 1969, doing "How Can I Be Sure." It wasn't as easy as it looked. It was pretty much a six-day rehearsal. We had to do five days of actual rehearsal, starting at eight am every morning. Then, on Saturday, we did the whole dress rehearsal, performing for a live audience. All of this was just to make sure everything went right for the "big show" on Sunday night.

We got two minutes of airtime for all that work. Okay, maybe a little more, but pretty much one, maybe two songs, tops. It was really rushed and chaotic. And Ed himself was never going to be mistaken for the warmest in the room. Frankly, I don't think he liked us very much—you know, the long hair and everything. It was pretty surreal, being in the theater I'd seen on television in my parents' home back in Pelham as a kid. This was the place where Elvis performed, and for all I knew, I was standing right on that very same place. Amazing. Some of my best memories involve meeting the many comedians who also performed on the shows. Fun, mainly kind and all interesting. Among them were Buddy Hackett, Alan King, Jackie Mason, Myron Cohen, Henny Youngman, the Smothers Brothers. All of these "giants" we either met through Sid Bernstein or by appearing on TV.

Alan King is one who especially comes to mind. When we did "Hullabaloo," there was a comedy sketch in with Alan playing a cop who was out to arrest these "rascals" who were disturbing the peace. Eddie, Gene, Dino, and I were all hunched down inside these barrels on the set. Alan was going around with a flashlight searching for us and blew a police whistle. Eddie then jumped up out of the barrel and the rest of us followed, going into "I Ain't Gonna Eat Out My Heart Anymore." When we finished, Alan "arrested" Eddie, dragging him off by the collar, saying he'd caught those Rascals and was going to drag Eddie off to the barbershop. It was all silly and we didn't know what we were doing. All we knew was we were having fun

There's something about comics and musicians. Even today it seems like comedians and musicians are both often fans of each other's work. Bill Murray, being one of my absolute favorites. In fact I still see him now and again at some of my shows. Like me, he's a massive baseball fan. Jerry Lewis was another comedian I remember meeting. I got to know him through his son, Gary Lewis, of Gary Lewis and the Playboys. We worked a lot with Gary on the road and I even see him sometimes on the road to this day. His father was hilarious, whether on stage or just one on one. We met all these guys and really clicked with some of them. It was familiar territory, harkening back to the days playing in the Catskills, where the resorts would always have comedians coming in and out every week.

It's fair to say that not all comedians embraced us. Once we started doing TV, there could sometimes be a little bit of distance between us and the older comics we'd be around backstage. I'm sure it was more a generational thing than anything else. There's one comedian—he's gone now, God rest his soul—of whom I was a big fan. I loved the guy, but he really wasn't a good person when we met him backstage at the Sullivan show. I won't name him because I don't want to be disrespectful, but it was a bummer, the man simply wasn't anywhere near the same person off stage than he was on—completely different person in real life. Fortunately, more often than not, I've found this to be the exception to the rule.

It's the same with professional athletes, I've come across over the years. Like me, I've noticed that many of my brethren became musicians because we just didn't have what it took to become athletes. I loved baseball and would have been a ballplayer if I could've been, but that was never going to happen. Many athletes who I've met feel a kinship toward musicians for the exact same reason. In the end we're all fans! Although a New York Yankees fan, one of my great thrills was meeting my boyhood idol, Willie Mays, probably the greatest player with a bat and a glove who ever lived. He was a great guy, so kind and generous with his time. Needless to say it shocked the hell out of me when he asked for my autograph. What an amazing world!

I remember so vividly the first time I heard Ray Charles. It was nothing short of thrilling listening to him playing the piano like that. His left hand so rhythmic, his right, so melodic. The chords made it sound like there were five, six, even seven instruments involved. Gospel and blues. Together. One was for church, and the other for saloons. Not many people were doing this at that time. It started a musical revolution that became rhythm and blues and led all the way to hip hop.

I knew I had to learn to play like that. One thing is for certain; Ray Charles was the reason I wanted to play piano. Being trained in the classics was one thing, but hearing Ray was a whole other thing. As I once told an interviewer, I shaped myself after Ray Charles. I idolized this man's music. I was fortunate that TV gave me the opportunity to play with him in the same room. It was on the "Joan Rivers Show," and Ray was a guest that night. I sat in with the show's band, the Hudson Brothers, and played during all the commercial breaks. Ray was over in the area where Joan Rivers interviewed people. I was singing and playing directly to him. I had my eyes on him for what seemed like the entire time. I could tell he was listening because when I'd do something he liked, he'd do this little thing with his head, kind of like nodding. I'll never forget it—the feeling that gave me. He had this really big smile on his face and was nodding his head to the beat. The great Ray Charles listening to me and, in my head at least, giving a little approval of my playing. Imagine how I felt later on learning that Ray, like Willie, was also a fan. Lord have mercy!

Meeting Sammy Davis, Jr. was yet another truly amazing moment. After viewing the Beatles videos of "Strawberry Fields Forever" and "Penny Lane."—both remaining brilliant to this day—it inspired us to produce videos of our own. Shortly thereafter we were asked to be on the "Joey Bishop Show." We were set up to do two songs and we really wanted to have our video play on air as we performed one of the songs. The producer of the show wouldn't let us do it. He refused to cut away from us. He flat-out denied us. Sammy Davis, Jr. came out of his dressing room, must've noticed how unhappy we were with this guy attempting to dismiss us like that. Sammy asked us to fill him in on what went down. Sammy listened and then smiled at us. We couldn't help but smile back. He said "Don't worry about it. I'll take care of it." We'd never met him before. The man didn't know us from Adam, but sure enough, Sammy Davis Jr. got them to play our video.

Talk about paying it forward. There's no doubt that Sammy had gone through his share of brutality in his days coming up. Everyday occurrences that would be hard for any of us to comprehend. What he saw… what he experienced… his harsh reality… It's beyond brutal just attempting to imagine. And here we were, four kids angry because some producer wouldn't play our video. And here he was, not trivializing it, not attempting to teach us a lesson on what he'd gone through. He simply gave us a kind smile so genuine that it made us smile in return. An absolute legend in so many ways, my gratitude and respect for that man have no boundaries!

That also goes to show that all the places where you perform, whether they're hotels, casinos, wherever, they're not all created equal. Honestly, what was true then is still pretty much true now, especially when it comes to the hotels where promoters will put you up. In our early days, we didn't really care about the accommodations and that was a good thing, especially for the promoters, who just want to get you a room in places that don't cost them a lot of money. I'm being pretty tactful here. Let's just say they're not "first-class." If you want to think "dumps," you wouldn't be far off. But it never really mattered to us; at least it didn't matter to me. We'd all double up in rooms, usually me and Eddie in one and Gene and Dino in another. We'd all lived together in a hotel up the street from Atlantic, so what difference did it make?

The first one in the group who made us aware that we should each have our own "suites" in first- class hotels was Gene. The rest of us, honestly, really didn't care. We just wanted to get to the show, get some rest, and get on to the next show. Of course, that was somewhat complicated by the fact that Eddie and Gene despised flying, so we did a fair amount of driving when we were out on the road. I say "we," but I usually was the driver and I could never begin to tell you how many miles I logged up and down the east coast while the other guys rested or slept. It was especially hard because I prefer flying, even to this day, even though it's much more difficult now than it was in the Rascals' day. We used to be able to drive right up onto the runway with all our gear, instruments, and all, and load it on to the plane. Today, we don't even bring our own instruments on the road because it's just too complicated with all the security and so on. The shows' promoters provide everything where we play, even that heavy Hammond B-3.

On the road, you play big places and small places, good places and bad, but you're still lucky to play at all. I'm grateful for the places I've been and the places I still go. So many stand out, but not always the ones you might expect.

Sometimes the shows that really stick in your mind years later are the ones that were way out of the way or presented unusual challenges or circumstances. Often, they're memorable because they involved bizarre situations. I had a good number of those with the Rascals and each of them stands out, either because of where they were or the others with whom we played. I'll tell you what—every time I might think for a split second that I might be a big deal; I remember the rodeo. I can't remember the exact date, but at the height of our popularity, with all those hit records and adoring fans, we came on stage following a rodeo at a fairground in Tampa, Florida. The night before there had been a rodeo in town on the very spot where we were about to play this outdoor show. The cleanup of the grounds had not exactly been, shall we say, expertly done. It wasn't the most pleasant situation, but we took the stage in the middle of a freshly manured cow pasture.

The show goes on despite the things that sometimes threaten to bring it all to a halt. We used to play a lot of college shows and I remember one, at Brown University, probably around 1967. I'm up there playing my Hammond B-3 on a riser behind the other guys, with my eyes closed and singing. I'm in my trance, inside the song. All of a sudden, I open my eyes and see a beer can flying toward the stage, right at Gene. I recall that he ducked and wasn't hurt. I remember thinking that we were playing pretty good, and remember wondering what the hell had Gene done…?

One time, during a Shea Stadium show we played in 1966, we were on a revolving stage so that everyone all around the ballpark could see us. Dino didn't take well to the movement and, at one point, fell right off the stage. That's just one example. I can't tell you the number of times we had to find our way to and from the stage in the dark. You have to remember that all over any stage are cables, wires, connectors, all the stuff that electrifies the instruments and amplifiers. Keep in mind that I had to get up on a riser toward the back of the stage where my Hammond sits. More than once, in the dark, I'd nearly kill myself tripping over and getting caught in a microphone or amp cable. It's bad enough that you're playing an instrument the size of a refrigerator, but it would be worse if that "refrigerator" fell over on you.

Everybody thinks, naturally, that we must always play in classy places and get provided with the best of everything—sound, lighting, dressing rooms, and great food. Not true. Sure, some places are better than others, but the Rascals had our share of less-than-ideal circumstances in which we had to perform. There was a show we played in Arizona with the Buffalo Springfield. Stephen Stills, David Crosby, both great singers and musicians who eventually became the core of Crosby, Stills, and Nash. It was another outdoor show, so they had to bring in electricity using long extension cords. That was one problem. The other was that they had no stage. Instead, two pickup trucks were brought in and parked back-to-back which served as our "stage."

Another particular show that stands out is one that we performed in Puerto Rico. Our songs, especially "Groovin,'" had such a Latin flavor, we became very popular in Puerto Rico. We were a huge hit there and, in the late '60s, became the first American rock group to play the island. You might be surprised to know the venue was a bullfighting arena. It was certainly a surprise to us! On the other hand, we'd never had a reception like that. Before the show they drove us around in a big convertible with the top down for the crowd to see us. They were cheering and we were waving. It was like we were bullfighters or something and the crowd really ate it up, but it was all a little strange to us.

There was another show we played where nobody came. I'm serious. NOBODY came. It was somewhere in North Carolina, and we were there to play with Neil Diamond and Iggy Pop. It was the worst show I can remember. We were out in the middle of nowhere, with no one there, but we had to play. Thinking back, I think the organizers were out to lose money on the deal, which they did. They seemed pretty happy to watch the show and see their money go up in smoke. I'll leave it to you to decide what their reasons might have been. Let's just say they could be the same people who want to make money on some things when the authorities aren't looking but lose money when they're being watched.

We became really good friends on the road with other touring bands at the time. Tommy James and the Shondells were one group we used to see a lot of on the road in the Rascals days. I still see him a fair amount when I play with my own band today. Tommy had some huge hits, with

"Crimson and Clover," "I Think We're Alone Now," "Mony, Mony," and, like me and all of the rest of us who have spent more than 10 minutes in the music business, knows first-hand how dirty a business it can be. He even wrote his own book about his interactions with some, shall we say, unsavory characters in the business titled "Me, the Mob, and the Music." More power to him. I'm just not sure I'd want to aggravate those guys. We all knew they were there in the background, but I'd prefer to leave them there. That's maybe how I made it to the age I am.

The Rascals never got involved with any of that stuff, mainly because our manager, Sid Bernstein, had an ex-school mate who kept an eye on us. Sid made sure we got paid, which is something that didn't happen for every rock and roll act in the '60s and '70s. There are hundreds of musicians from back in the day who sold millions of records and hardly saw a dime. Those behind the scenes running the record companies would sometimes manipulate the writer's credits so they could get the publishing money, even though they weren't even in the room when a song was written. Was that fair? No. But there are a lot of things about the music business— remember, it's a business—that aren't fair, still to this day. Are you getting the idea that Felix was growing up? I was, but I've never lost my idealism.

So much of what we thought of as music really had become more about show business. I'll give you an example. When the Monkees came along, they were kind of different because, for one thing, they had their own TV show. The TV show was really the whole reason they existed.

They weren't a band in the same sense that we were. The Monkees pretty much were meant to capitalize on the success of the Beatles' first movie, "A Hard Day's Night." Michael Nesmith, Peter Tork, the late Davey Jones, and Mickey Dolenz—weren't exactly conventional, as I said, in that they weren't really a band that came up together. They were put together by producers. Because of that, they took a lot of heat for not playing their own instruments. In many ways, their path contrasted with that of the Rascals and probably has a lot more in common with performers of today. The Rascals played the clubs and schools long before we ever did concert halls and arenas. We cut our teeth in those places, more like Springsteen and musicians like that. The Monkees really started at the top, like some of today's artists do. They were a media creation—and they got paid big-time like their counterparts of today do.

In Tommy James' book, he talks about how, at the height of their popularity, the Monkees got either $100,000 or 100 per cent of the ticket sales per show just to show up. That meant promoters lost money, but they increased their reputations, so they could go on to promote bigger and bigger artists—at least that's what Tommy says. We never got those kinds of deals, but then again, we didn't have a TV show, and we really didn't fully invest in the whole video craze. We were, after all, "pre-MTV." The Rascals flirted with making videos because the Beatles did so, and we looked up to them. But we never got our own TV show. There is one video out there on the Internet of "Good Lovin'" that really is advanced for its time. If you look closely, you'll even see a young Denzel

Washington featured in it. Pretty cool! Getting back to the Monkees, let's face it. A lot of today's groups share a lot more in common with them than with the Rascals. They've never played in a club, but that's mainly because there's not a lot of opportunity to do so anymore. Clubs don't hire live musicians because they don't have to, due to all the recorded options out there. So, kids get known by doing a YouTube video and that spreads their reputation. The Monkees, following the Beatles, did the same thing with their videos, but they had the added bonus of their TV show. That was genius and probably one reason they can come back every now and then to do a tour. In 2016, I hosted a show on Sirius radio to mark their 50th anniversary and to kick off their reunion tour. I'm happy for them, really for anyone who keeps going. I also have to admit that I found myself wishing the Rascals would have made it to our own 50th anniversary tour, but more on that later.

During our touring days, the Rascals would see a ton of other groups on the road. We used to kind of be rivals with the Lovin' Spoonful in the '60s, but sometimes we'd work together, and to this day, I consider John Sebastian a good friend. In the '60s, we were all pretty much in competition with one another to have the next big "hit." Now, in our seventies, we're all very friendly with each other. I mean, don't get me wrong; it's not like we were fighting with the other groups on the charts at the time, but John remembers those days this way: "You have to understand the real truth about the '60s and the truth is groups weren't all friendly and chummy and love is going to find a way kind of an attitude.

It was competition. It wasn't just friendly, ha, ha, I'll slap you on the back and I'll lend you my drummer anytime kind of thing. It was intense."

My relationship with John goes all the way back to those days playing at the Metropole in New York. John and Zal Yanofsky, the Lovin' Spoonful's lead guitarist, came to see me and Dino play there. He recalls that, as the door opened to the club, there was this sound coming out that sounded like a train coming toward them; it was really loud. It was just the two of us that John heard: just me and Dino, no one else. He describes the experience as so "intense" and recalled that I was just "playing the hell out that thing," meaning the Hammond B-3. John jokingly describes it as the day he and Zal got the "bad news."

John paid us a great compliment, saying he turned to Zal and said something like "We're just going to have to practice every day to get anywhere near this good." That's John's story, so it's fine with me, although I don't necessarily agree with the part of it where he says they had to practice harder. I will agree that once the Rascals got going, we did kind of have what John describes as an "understanding" with the Spoonful. It started out as a joke, but there was also some seriousness to it. "Uptown" Manhattan was soul music and downtown was folk music. I used to tell John that the Spoonful "owned" everything below 14th Street and we "owned" everyplace else. John says the Rascals were really an inspiration to the Spoonful. The truth is we really kind of inspired each other.

John and I have kept up our friendship to this day; he's an amazing storyteller and someone with whom I've worked many times. There's a video on YouTube showing us together in 1984. It was a TV show called "Deja Vue" that John hosted. I have great memories of that show. John and I did "You Better Run" together. It's also memorable because it was the last time I saw Joe Cocker. He was amazing. Here's what I remember: We were rehearsing until approximately eleven pm, and we had a six am call the next day to tape the show. Joe was so drunk that he could hardly even open his lower jaw, but at six o'clock in the morning he showed up and he was perfect! I asked him how in the hell he did it. "Takes a lot of practice, mate," he said in his glorious cockney accent. Practice or not, I couldn't understand how he was able to go. God bless him.

One reason the Spoonful and the Rascals got along as well as we did—and the same is true of our relationship with Tommy James and the Shondells, and so many others— is that we all came out of the same era. There were some overlapping eras going on musically at the time. This was at the end of what you might call the "Peppermint Twist" era, named for a song which I had performed so many times with Joey Dee, and the beginning of rock and roll that was centered more in rhythm and blues. John and the Spoonful were into the old blues, with players as he says that didn't have the "songbook" (meaning repertoire) of the old black artists like we did, but the Spoonful still went back to roots music, following traditions ranging from jug bands to country artists like Buck Owens. It was a period of discovery, looking back to artists a generation or two before and not just listening to or following the beat of our contemporaries. The fact is all of us at that time took part in reinventing what rock was, and what it would become, borrowing a lot from the "masters" and making it our own.

Speaking of the Spoonful, I remember we worked a show with them at the old New York Coliseum. Strange how low the ticket prices were back in those days. I think we're talking around $3.50 to see both bands. John still has a ticket from a show we did with the Spoonful in 1969 at the University of Massachusetts, Amherst, where the ticket price was even less: $2.00. Can you imagine? I remember that show at the New York Coliseum so vividly—and it has nothing to do with music. That night Eddie went onstage with his "fly" down. I'm not sure if he knew, but the crowd noticed it right away and started cheering, even before he sang his first lyric, and they kept at it in all the wrong spots of the songs. Finally, Eddie looked down and realized why the ladies were focused a bit lower than his high notes.

There were so many people we met in those days, and they all had their own talents. It's no wonder the kids today look back on a lot of these musicians as legends. They were. Let's start with James Brown. When it came to performing, no one was better at doing a show. James Brown was someone I always emulated. Our manager, Sid Bernstein, was friends with James' manager, who, one morning phoned me on short notice and asked, "How'd you like to open for James Brown at Madison Square Garden tomorrow night? " Come on, you're killing me. Open for James Brown?

That's not the kind of thing you say no to. So we did it and I was blown away by the spectacle, by the audience's reaction to him. I said to the band, "We should do some of this; we ought to put some of this kind of stuff in our shows." And with that we began adding some of the showmanship we'd learned from performers like Little Richard. Out of that show and others, by watching performers at that level, we made our shows better, more exciting, more theatrical. It not only improved our musicianship, but it improved our performance skills. It was such an evolving era, one in which I remain ever honored to be part of.

Although the Rascals played colleges and big arenas, we never really left behind our roots in the clubs. Two of the biggest clubs we played were on the west coast: the Whiskey A Go Go and the Filmore West. These were huge steps for us as artists, but also took us way out of our east coast comfort zone. The Whiskey a Go Go opened in 1964 and is still operating in Los Angeles to this day. It was a great launching pad for bands, and our management booked us in both places as a way to solidify us as being not just an east coast band. It was important to unite the east and the west coasts if you wanted to have number one records; it wasn't enough just to be big on one coast and unknown on the other. You had to be big in both or your success was limited. So, in 1966 we played the Whiskey for the first time and broke all attendance records there, doing a full week of shows during the last week of January that year. It was unbelievable. The lines went around the block, it felt like a five-minute walk just to get in line. Our sell-out record held for a couple years until Otis Redding broke it in 1968.

The Filmore was another story. In many ways it presented us with a kind of culture clash. The place was known for groups like Jefferson Airplane, the Grateful Dead, the whole San Francisco psychedelic crowd. Those were some of the bands we played with at the Filmore. One time was with the Doors in June of 1967, then again in 1968, along with jazz man Charles Lloyd and his quartet, in addition to some people from the cast of the show "Hair." That place was like a den of Hippies. It was strange. Bill Graham, the genius who ran it, made the Filmore a place that featured some of the most excellent sound and lighting found anywhere. And then you'd enter the dressing room, and it was like entering a different dimension of both space and time. Strange sights. I remember one time there were wolf cubs—I'm not kidding—wolf cubs being kept in a crevice in the dressing room wall. I have no idea why. I didn't ask.

When we played with the Doors at the Filmore, I spent some time backstage with Jim Morrison. Because I make a rule about never saying negative things about people, I won't say a lot about him, except that he was not especially a "sweetheart" around other people. He was out of control the one time I saw him at the Filmore. That was my experience, but I really didn't know him well at all, except for that one gig.

The West Coast scene was out of control, so insane. People would come into the club costumed-out, Superman, Alice in Wonderland, in their own little worlds, dancing with themselves, spinning around, completely gone, drugged out of their minds. It was as if the colors of a kaleidoscope infused our world. It was madness—total madness, bordering on a zombie-like form that infused ridiculous, over-the-top amounts of drug use with freedom of expression. There were times when the entire scene felt like an experimental horror film. Then it all stopped. When Ronald Reagan became governor of California, the hippies that went to these clubs were put on notice. I remember I went out there with Smokey Robinson; we were in a hotel, and all of our shows had been canceled because the clubs were temporarily shut down. As far as many of the residents in nearby Beverly Hills were concerned, the new governor was little more than the new sheriff in town, and that's when the "movement" moved up to Haight Ashbury in San Francisco, far away from the folks in Beverly Hills who let Reagan know that changes weren't about to come to their neighborhoods.

Smokey and I spent a little time hanging around during this temporary sound blackout. He'd constantly ask if I played cards. He was always trying to put one over on unsuspecting card players. But I wasn't about to lose my money to any card shark, especially one as smooth as Smokey Robinson. I remember not long after that, we were playing with Smokey up in Boston, Harvard Square, I think. He was opening for us, and I always felt a little funny about that. Here's a guy who's a monster in our business, such a great, great talent and he's opening for us? I remember—maybe to ease the strangeness I felt in his performing first—telling him how much we loved and respected his music. Smokey thought for a second and came back with, "You play cards?" I laughed before thankfully turning the subject back to music. It was almost a nightly occurrence, performers, working musicians, playing shows, making money, and then playing cards with those who are far more experienced. Men who knew the intricacies of separating an artist's cash from his wallet.

We played on a tour called the Dick Clark Cavalcade of Stars Tour. He'd arrange these tours with busloads of singers and groups with chart-topping records. The tour was a big deal to us as it helped to solidify an audience in the south. We were going to towns I'd never heard of, and the people loved us, so we always had a solid foundation of support. In fact, we met so many people that one of them was even my first wife. I met her while on that tour, when we were in Alabama. Eddie, Gene, Dino, and I went to these little towns like Hazard, Kentucky and Waycross, Georgia. I'd never even heard of these towns. Playing those kinds of small towns really helped establish our reputations, especially in the "Deep South." Energetic crowds who loved what we were doing.

So, we were on this tour, the "Dick Clark Cavalcade," and with us were Paul Revere and the Raiders, B.J. Thomas and the Triumphs, a whole lot of acts who, like us, had hit records at the time. It really was a lot of fun, but it also had a serious side. On that particular tour, I believe it was, we were between Miami and Tampa, Florida, when we almost got killed. Instead of going on the bus, we decided to rent an RV and follow the bus. The idea was that if we wanted to go off and take in the countryside, we could do that with the RV and catch up with the tour bus later. Dino would say things like, "Let's pull over. Let's stop here." What a great idea.

Well, Gene went on the bus, which turned out to be the smart choice. However, that's where he lost all his money because the guys started playing cards. Like I said, when you're on the road and someone, anyone asks if you play cards, always say no! Empty wallet Gene, though, turned out to be the lucky one in the end. It was a Saturday night. The RV broke down in Ft. Pierce, Florida. We found a place to eat, walked in and quickly realized our bad decision. Our hair, our clothes, American soldiers our age fighting in Vietnam… I guess some of that didn't sit too well with a group of bikers who chose not to be among our band's target audience. In fact they straight took umbrage at every drop of our every being. We ended up needing a police escort just to escape from that place safely. And the cops weren't really that happy to be helping out a bunch of guys who looked like us. To this day, the memory reminds me of the movie "Easy Rider." This really happened. We had to be escorted out of town.

Playing in the south in those days wasn't the only place where you had to step carefully, and all the danger didn't come from protests or threats. Some of it was right there in front of you before and after you played on stage. There were always people around who would hand you stuff, like a glass with some mystery component inside. People would just want to do something for you, like, at least once, I remember a girl coming up to me backstage at the Filmore and saying, "I can make clothes for you." She did, and they were fantastic. There were always people around offering to do something for you. That kind of stuff was always going on, with women coming and going. Sometimes they just wanted to grab on to you, pull at you, both when you were onstage and offstage. The other thing that the Filmore shared with so many places we played was that you had to make your own way to the stage. Nobody with flashlights guiding you in those days. It was at the Filmore that I fell onto a Leslie speaker and thought I'd broken every bone in my body. Fortunately, that wasn't the case.

That incident points out a big difference between then and now. Back then, we didn't have road managers all the time like I do now. That would have been helpful in terms of just getting us to where we needed to be, both the venue and the stage. My current road manager, Caesar Sabatini, sometimes tells people he's there to "babysit" me on the road, and he's probably not far off.

There's stuff today that I, that we, the Rascals, used to have to do ourselves—carrying equipment, setting it up, checking sound are just a few. Today, that's all done by professionals. We used to be our own crew. We had no choice. Times have changed, mostly for the better.

I'm still amazed at the number of impressive, if not important, places the Rascals played in our time together. Some of them stand out for historical reasons. I've already mentioned Madison Square Garden, the old Garden, which closed in 1968, which was without question one of the greatest places you'd ever want to play. We played there a number of times, including having the privilege of playing the last show in that building, closing it down, together with Aretha Franklin, Sonny and Cher, Joe Tex, and our old friend from Atlantic, King Curtis. It was in May of that year, at a tribute concert to Martin Luther King, Jr., who had been shot and killed the previous month. It was a special night for an immeasurably special man, who had a lot to do with so much of what I believe about social justice and equality. It was a wonderful show in which I was honored and privileged to take part.

Not only did we play the last show at the old Madison Square Garden, we also closed down the old RKO Theater in New York. We actually played there a number of times. The one I remember most was sharing the bill with The Who and Cream. A great line-up closing down an amazing venue. I think that one thing that helped us play so many great theaters and halls was the relationship we had with our fans. We had built a special bond that's nearly impossible to put into words, as it's more a feeling, a sensation that fills me with such overwhelming pleasure.

It wasn't long before we began traveling the world, performing in most countries, including England, Sweden, Germany, France, and throughout Europe. One experience we had while touring Europe really stands out in my memory. We were doing the Tom Jones television show in 1969. We did two songs with him, one of them was "Midnight Hour," and I really had a ball singing with him, it was a great show. Tom was great.

The first experience I had with Tom goes back long before the European tour of 1969. It was when he came to see us play at the Phone

Booth in New York. At that time, I was seeing this very attractive blonde who was there in the audience. Tom Jones unequivocally personified the term 'sex symbol,' women went bonkers for the man. Anyway, I saw him go over and dance with my girlfriend, and I said to myself, "Goodbye. It was nice while it lasted." Well, you know what? When Tom found out she was my girlfriend, he found a couple of other women to "dance with." I knew immediately that Tom was a "bro." Here was a man who respected other people's lives. He's a mensch. That really made an impression on me. He could have swept her off her feet, but he didn't. To this day, I say, "Yes, sir, Mr. Jones. Very cool." It's this memory that has stuck in my mind every time I've seen him in person or performance. The man is a legend in so many more ways than one.

There's the need for consensus when you're in a band, and traveling was an area of constant struggle within the Rascals. There were several parts of the world that, for various reasons, we all failed to agree on going. We were invited to play in Vietnam, but Gene wouldn't go, so that didn't happen. I've always regretted that. We could have gone to Japan, but, again, not everyone in the group agreed.

We did however, all agree on performing in Hawaii. All four of us loved Hawaii. So much so that it practically became a second home. Hawaiians made us feel welcome as if we were relatives, and we, in turn, fell in love with the people and their islands, going there multiple times almost every year between 1965 and 1972, often taking family members along with us. I'll always cherish the memories of being there with my sister Fran and my dad, who had been there during the war and never got to experience the Hawaii that we had. It was special to see my father have a good time.

Eddie brought his whole family. Eddie's mom was from a very poor background. She had always dreamt of going and the memory of watching her enjoying herself still brings tears to my eyes. Just seeing how much joy being there in Hawaii brought to her and their family was special.

Being a family affair, it seemed we always brought at least one Italian woman along with us who insisted on cooking. Sometimes it was my Aunt Emma, and I remember what she had to go through to come up with the ingredients to make us some of her Italian specialties. She'd go all over the place looking for her items to make us a real Italian meal. I smile when I think about Aunt Emma taking all these lovely little Japanese ladies all over town looking for the stuff she needed and the satisfaction she got from tracking it down and bringing it back to our table. Those were great, great days that inspired so much music out of us, including the song "My Hawaii which we put out on our "Once Upon a Dream" album in 1968.

We'd sometimes go there to play alone but sometimes worked with other big groups from that era. We played Honolulu with Tommy James and the Shondells among them where we stayed at the foot of Diamond Head in a couple of old, turn of the century hotels, us in one and Tommy and his band in the other. As Tommy puts it, "Felix was always one major hit ahead of me. While the Rascals were working together, we were working different sides of the street. We had many of the same fans."

George Harrison had a home in Hawaii, and I spent some time with him on an occasion or two. I got a sense of what it's like to operate in that stratosphere. Only those four guys could know what it was really like, but I remember saying to George, "The Beatles are so big that if one of you takes two steps to the right it's like the whole earth tips along with him." He agreed with my joke, so there must have been some truth to it. He then went on to express a little bit about what a heavy burden it was for them. They really couldn't go anywhere or do the kinds of things that the rest of us take for granted. I toured with Ringo in later years as part of his All-Star band, and to this day—nearly 50 years after the Beatles breakup—if Ringo wants to see a movie, he has to rent out the theater. Normality for those four men became an absolute impossibility the moment they became the Fab Four. In the eyes of the world, they had become Beatles first, and people second.

John Lennon was an interesting person. A man very much in touch with his art, as well as his position within its world. I never really got to know him well but did meet him one time and he left me, to be honest, a little unsettled. We were introduced, and I was talking, and he was just looking at me. I kept talking and he just kind of kept staring in my direction. When the "conversation" ended, I said to one of his people, a manager, I guess, that I didn't think John liked me or that he was the slightest bit interested in what I was saying. The guy laughed and said "That's just John. He can't see you." What? It turns out that John was very near-sighted, and he didn't have his glasses on at the time. He was just staring because I must have been out of focus. I was assured by his "people," though, that he was listening. I'll never know if he was or wasn't.

If there's anyone who loves being on stage, who loves performing more than Ringo Starr, I don't think I've met them. He loves it! For him it's a passionate love affair that rings as intense today as it did 60 years ago. Getting out there in front of the audience is what he lives for, and he'll probably keep doing it until the very last day of his life. He's a terrific drummer who has only gotten better over the years. A gifted singer he is not. And that's a sensitive subject for Ringo, so let's just keep this between us.

I was on tour with him as part of this all-star band (he called it, naturally, his All-Starr Band) in 1995. It was a kind of super group concept; others were Randy Bachman of Guess-Who and Bachman-Turner Overdrive; Mark Farner of Grand Funk; Mark Rivera, the sax player from Billy Joel's Band; the late Billy Preston, and the late John Entwistle of the Who, along with Ringo's son, Zak, who also plays drums.

I love the fact that Ringo is so human that he can actually be hurt by what others think of him. So, we're playing one night, I'm pretty sure it was in Boston, and that morning a review came out in the local paper panning Ringo's singing. We were all backstage, in the dressing room with Ringo waving the newspaper as if it were on fire. Nobody knew what to say. What do you say to a Beatle who's upset? Probably nothing is the answer. I remember him questioning no one, in particular, asking out loud, "Can you believe this bloke wrote I can't sing?" Everybody got quiet.

I spoke up, probably stupidly. "Come on, bro, you're Ringo. You can sing anyway you want." The room got quieter, no doubt awaiting the explosion. Instead, Ringo looked at me and said something like, "Okay, if you can say that, why can't this bloke? What's he know about it?" Point made. Ringo is like most of us. He'll take criticism, but only from people who in his mind know what the hell they're talking about.

That raises the idea that, when you're a musician and you meet people in the business, you meet them on a different level than people who aren't in the business. The attitude among us is like, "Hey, I like what you do." It's nice because sometimes you're the only people who really can understand each other. You kind of know what the other person is going through because you've been there. So, when you meet people like Bruce Springsteen and members of U-2, it's more than just a casual meeting. You really get to know them, and they respect what you do and you respect what they do. Springsteen not only loved "People Got to be Free," like I said, but he tells the story that the first rock concert he ever went to was a Rascals show at a roller rink in New Jersey. Coincidentally, if you believe in coincidences, Steve Van Zandt, who became part of Bruce's E-Street Band, was there that same night, and neither of them knew it until the subject of "What was your first rock concert?" came up years later.

Being Italian-American, I looked up to all those vocal groups from the '50s, many of whom had Italian roots, among them Frankie Valli and the Four Seasons. Frankie was always somebody I enjoyed listening to and getting to know. Dion DiMucci of Dion and the Belmonts was another

Italian success story in rock and roll who made an impression. Dion gave me a lot of solid advice in my early days, like staying out of different clubs that certain people owned or controlled. He and the Belmonts, like Frankie and the Four Seasons, had some serious harmony going on. Frankie is still working and lives in California now, so I see him every so often. He's a good friend, and ours is a friendship that I've valued greatly over the years.

Jimi Hendrix is someone else whom I knew way back before he became the Jimi Hendrix whose image we'd recognize for the remainder of human kind. Jimi worked with Joey Dee for a while, so we shared that in common. He was also part of the whole New York scene, even playing for a while, I believe, with the Isley Brothers. It was upon taking off in England where a lot about him changed. When he came back, he did one of his first shows in America in Central Park with the Rascals. He opened up for us, and I remember seeing him backstage. Jimi was tall, very lean, and back in the day had been very shy, nothing at all like he was on stage. All of a sudden, I see him in the dressing room, all decked out with colors, a broad-brimmed black hat on, he looked like he had feathers on him. I said, "Hey, what happened to you, Jimi? What's going on?" It felt as if he'd been reborn. Seriously. Jimi went from being a kind of bent-over, shy guitarist who was like, "Excuse me, I'm going to play a solo now," to someone who truly seemed to have found himself, someone who really had it together. I told him how great I thought he looked. "What happened?"

"I got my shit together now," he said with the confidence of the performer we'd all become so familiar with in the coming months.

What happened…? In England and all these incredible guitarists like Jimmy Page and Jeff Beck, and Eric Clapton, all these monster guitar players came to hear Jimi playing downtown and thought he was unbelievable. Here they were, these monsters of rock guitar who recognized instantly that this young upstart was light years ahead of anyone they'd ever heard. From there, it became the Jimi Hendrix Experience, and he put that record out. All of a sudden, his confidence level as a human being, because he had a tough life, was entirely different. When he went out there, and he played that night, it was as if somebody had attached a missile to him. He soared.

I remember it was Gene, I think, who got a little like, "Hasn't he been on a long time?" I think Gene was a little overwhelmed. After that, Jimi did his first real tour with the Monkees and Mickey Dolenz told me about Jimi, that the kids were really scared of his playing." I can understand because he was so forceful. It was just the opposite of who he was in life and who he was before crossing the pond. He went away and came back a mega-star. He just exploded.

He was such a generous person. In fact, Jimi once gave me his watch. We were just hanging out backstage. He noticed me noticing his watch. He took it off his wrist, admired it a moment as if saying goodbye, and said, "Here, I want you to have this." Just like that. I attempted to dissuade him, but he wouldn't take no for an answer, just repeating that he wanted me to have it. It took me a couple of minutes before realizing I wasn't going to win this round.

As our relationship continued, and Jimi's drug use became a concern, our lawyer, who was also Jimi's lawyer, asked me if maybe I could help Jimi out, help get him off the drugs. I tried, but in reality, it was like trying to control an ocean's tide, sadly too far beyond my abilities. It wasn't long after that I saw Jimi at a concert in Madison Square Garden. He was so far gone. He took my arm and I had to help him to the dressing room and get him to sit down for about a half hour because he was so out of it. It's a sad story, but unfortunately not such an uncommon one in our world. Jimi's addiction took hold of him and so many in and around his ecosystem, and in the end, sadly, many of them found their actions and fates aligned with Jimi's. Hope you're sleeping well, special one!

We've had so many great artists leave us way too soon and there quite simply are no words for how profound their losses are. Learning of Prince dying a few years ago brought back so much of the pain I'd felt in losing those who I'd built relationships with throughout the '60s. His, like their lives, cut all too short. Prince was a freaking genius. He was a brilliant guitarist, a fantastic producer—someone who could do it all. I saw him at Madison Square Garden in 2011 and he had a flamboyance unlike most anyone I'd ever seen. He held the entire arena in the palm of his hand. His music, an absolute brilliant library of songs speaks for itself. It was fun to learn, though not surprising of the musical influences that we shared. Legends like Marvin Gaye and Sam Cooke, of which he truly became a peer.

Michael Jackson is another who we've lost far too soon. I'm not sure who, if anyone, is challenging him as a frontman in Heaven right now. Michael is surely one of the great, if not greatest, performers this world has ever seen. There's no question that he was aware of his standing within the Pentium of performers as I once saw Michael in a recording studio, and he'd had the record company build a runway from his dressing room to the spot in the studio where the microphone was situated. All around him—on his approach to his microphone—he had posters and photos hung of his heroes, his idols. Surrounded by the greatest artists of all time, he used that runway to reach the exact spot where he'd record.

Snow Day

9 yrs old

16 years old

16 yrs old

2020 version of a band meeting

A true honor

All that hair!

At least WE were smiling!

At the Barge in the Hamptons

Christina, Laura, and Aria

Dinner with Team Felix

Groovin

Dr. Felix V.

Family cruise 1954

Fran and the girls at the R&R HOF

Laura Cavaliere

Look at that lineup!

Man, we were tight!

Musicians HOF 2019

My beautiful bride on our wedding day

My beautiful little girls

My Guru Swami Satchidananda

My happy place

My brother Gene 2018 tour

Family & Rascals

Playing guitar at age 15

Predators game with friends from the band Sixwire

Rehearsal at the Nashville Symphony

Swingin 6

Syracuse University 1961

The perfect evening!

The Stereos 1959

The very Young Rascals

With Alice Cooper

With Aria and the band at the Nashville Symphony show

With Billy Joel at MSG

With Christina, Aria, Lisa, and Laura

With Dad and Eddie

Last picture ever of these Rascals

With Donna at the US Open

With Eddie and our girls

With Frankie Valli and Dion

With Gene, Tommy James, and Carmine Appice

With granddaughters Gemma and Gia

With John Sebastian

With Leo, Malia, and Christina

With Lisa and Donna

With Mark Rivera and Billy Joel

With my sister Fran and hubby Joe

With Obi and Gene

With Steve Cropper

With Swamiji, Theresa and girls

With the band! John, Vinnie, Benny, and Mike

With Lisa and Grandson Jonathan

2 years old

Chapter 6: Swami Satchidananda

◆

Career-wise, my life was on track. Music had called me, it truly inspired me down to the bones, to the point where I couldn't live without it. Performing, sharing that magical sense of brotherhood with both band and audience was nothing short of spiritual. But it was that same sense of spirituality that was missing in my personal life. I was in search of answers, something to fill that sense of how such a devout woman—such as my mom—who chose to live her life in absolute accordance with her faith—be taken in the prime of her life.

My constant search led me down several paths, led me through the readings of many books, encompassing many voices. I needed answers, perhaps, more importantly, a direction. I needed something to help fill this void of understanding. I had just finished reading "Autobiography of a Yogi" by Paramahansa Yogananda and found myself enchanted with the openness with which this Holy man attempted to share his life.

One day, a gentleman named Steve Paul, who owned a club in New York City called the Scene reached out and asked if we could help him out. He was hoping that the Rascals would perform for a TV pilot filmed at his club for a show on WNEW, Channel 5 in New York. To give you an idea, this place was like something from another planet, including Tiny

Tim being the house M.C. It was a popular place where most of the major acts played. The Scene was exactly that, on stage and off, recognizable faces everywhere. People like Jimi Hendrix, the Velvet Underground, Jose Feliciano, and so many more.

We walked into the club and heading toward the dressing room, I noticed a circle of young people surrounding a man in an orange robe, his hair down his back, his beard to his waist. I stopped. I just stopped. The moment was as instant as it was profound. I stood there, eyeing thing man in this circle of people who were hanging on his every word. It felt like only hours ago that I turned the final page and closed "Autobiography of a Yogi," and here I was staring at an actual Swami! My feet flowed me into this side room as the rest of the band continued to our dressing room.

I needed to meet this gentleman. So, I dropped everything and got in line with everybody else to get closer to this man captivating an entire room just by his presence. The way it worked was, you approached this holy man standing within the center of the circle and you kneeled down, he'd touch your head and then you'd move on. It was like a blessing. If you wanted to say something, you said something. If not, you just moved on.

As my turn approached, I found myself standing in front of this holy man and looking deep into his eyes. It was like I was looking up at the sky, at the seashore, a blast of spirituality that completely froze me. And I just kept staring into his eyes as I got closer and closer until he finally felt the need to enlighten me to the fact that I was holding up the line.

I was awestruck. Looking into his eyes, it was all open territory. I finally came out of it and made my way toward the dressing room. I remember feeling like my ego was crushed, thinking to myself that he's just a guy. What the hell was I doing? Why'd I make such a fool of myself standing there frozen like that in front of everyone in the room? But with all that banter going on inside my head, I knew that I had to speak with him.

Believe it or not, my next chance to meet this very eminent man came in the bathroom. I tracked him down and that's where we next met. Like I said, I was in search. So, when I walked into the bathroom, he was washing his hands very slowly, very deliberately. I could feel this kind of warmth. It was amazing the kind of feeling I got. It felt like everything had slowed down. It was similar to when you were a little kid and you just felt safe in your home. That's exactly the way it felt: safe.

I didn't know what to say. So, there he was washing his hands, and I said, "Excuse me. Uh, I'd really like to talk to you." What a great opening for a rock star, huh? Wow. So, he looked at me and kind of busted my chops a little bit. He looked straight at me, straight into my eyes. "Oh, you would, would you?"

"Yes," I said with a huge sense of sincerity. "I really would." So, he gave me a phone number. It was in some kind of script or something. He told me that was his phone number and that I should call him up anytime I wanted. He had a smile on his face, and I thought, he's joking with me. He's really toying with me. I knew he was. But everything he was doing was intended to throw me a little off-balance, knock my ego out. It really shakes you up and gets you off your game. That's the point. Now, he could talk to me, one on one.

Why? Swamis are just very happy, very free people. They have no burdens on their lives. They're just happy people. That really hit me. Can you imagine? I needed to know why and how a person could find himself in such a confused state. It took me about two weeks to get up enough nerve to call that number. But I did, and it led to an amazing, if not monumental, life-altering meeting with the Swami. It was the beginning of a long relationship, one that would lead me to refer to Swami Satchidananda, to this day, as "Swamiji," a term of respect and reverence.

I had a mountain of thoughts and reasons on why I wanted, actually felt the need, to talk with the Swami. He didn't have any idea of who I was or what I did with the Rascals and that was important. It's not like he knew about our #1 songs, our television appearances, our constant play on radio stations around the world, and he wouldn't have cared if he did. That wasn't what Swamiji Satchidananda was all about and that's exactly why I wanted to orbit his world. It's exactly how my new path in life began. This man was a holy, spiritual man, yes, but, at his most basic, he was simply a man who could teach me a new way to live my life. I believed he could because he had transformed his own and the lives of so many others.

It began here in the U.S. when Swamiji Satchidananda helped a famous movie producer who was very successful in the 1960s. He was very celebrated, but he had a drinking problem that affected him to the point where his family sent him to India to get cleaned up. During this process, he ran into Swamiji and got help without going to any hospitals or having any other treatment. The producer was so appreciative, he said to Swamiji, "I want to introduce you to my friends. I want to send you all around the world." As I was told the story, Swamiji really didn't want to go, but his own teacher told him, "You have to go. You have a gift. You can share our teachings with everybody because you have a personality. You can teach people." So, he went. Wherever they sent him, he didn't stay in a hotel. He stayed with a family. He went everywhere. He went to Paris; he traveled all over the world. And then he came to New York.

When he got to New York, he met Peter Max, the famous artist. Peter, at that time, was a young artist, who with his wife and family, lived a quintessentially bohemian lifestyle. Even though he was a hippie and maybe because of it, this guru, this saint, came to live in his house. He had no idea of the protocol for how to treat a holy man. He didn't know anything. Peter would invite all his friends in New York to his house to meet Swamiji. He'd tell everybody, "You have to come over and meet this Holy Man. This is really, really an excellent human being." So, my meeting with Swamiji was one of many he had with like-minded people—artists, performers, anxious and over-stressed executives.

That first time I spent with Swamiji was pretty simple, but monumental. Like I said before, I was raised Catholic back in Pelham and my mother was extremely devout. In the Catholic Church, there's confession, so I kind of started out that way with Swamiji. He offered me some tea, we sat down, and he asked what it was that I was looking for. I told him quite simply and honestly that I was mixed up, a little lost and was hoping that he might be willing to help me out. All the while, here I am with Eddie, Gene, and Dino traversing the world. We're stars. We're the Rascals, rocking and rolling with hits all over the place. What did I have to be unhappy about?

But like I said, I struggled to get over the question: what kind of God would take a person who went to church every day and leave the rest of us here? It just didn't make sense. It's like you're holy and it doesn't mean anything. I really needed an answer. Unfortunately, every time I asked, no one would even attempt to truly answer. All any one up to that point would tell me was that it's all just a part of the grieving process, a period for you to work through, and allow time to heal your pain.

That's all anybody really offered me in terms of figuring out the first "big" question I'd been keeping inside me for a long time: Why did my mother, this wonderful, spiritual woman, have to die at such a young age? That wasn't good enough. I told people I really wanted to know why. It sent me searching for answers, and the ones I was hearing just weren't getting me anywhere close to what I needed. I was an adult, I had a mind of my own, I was building a strong foundation of the man I saw growing myself into, but in many ways, I was still that same thirteen-year-old kid who watched his mother drift so painfully from this earth. Meeting Swamiji was the first light I had seen in a very longtime.

The second question really had to do with what I do for a living, the whole rock and roll industry. Even at such a young age—I was in my early twenties when I met Swamiji—I sensed a real difference between what my father did for work and what I ended up doing as a musician. My dad was a professional man, a dentist. He could put that sign up out front of his office, "DDS," and he was a dentist. He'd be a dentist the rest of his life. I'm a rock and roll entity. I make my money from something that I always knew could be over at any time. I'm only as good as my latest record. I could be gone tomorrow. If I didn't have a hit, I was—or at that time, we, the Rascals, were—history. I realized that, even at so young an age. And that really threw me.

Swamiji had asked me whether I realized how fortunate I was despite my success. I didn't have an answer. But he did. "Most people don't arrive at the point where you are until they're very old," he said. "It doesn't matter. You're a doctor; you're a lawyer. It doesn't matter. There's no stability anywhere on this planet and that's why you're here." He told me that, as I got older, I'd speak to people in other professions, and they would confirm what he had just said. I was fortunate, said Swamiji, because I'd gotten a jump on it.

"So, I'm really lucky that I'm miserable at a younger age? Is that what you're telling me?"

"What if I could give you a pill, and you'd have all this knowledge, all this consciousness?" he asked. "I bet you'd take it."

I told him I'd take it in a minute. "Yeah, Americans always want something that works fast, something they can have to fix things right now. There's no pill. What you have to do is you have to join a system, a method." But, before I did anything, he told me, number one, he wanted me to come to exercise classes, what they call hatha yoga. I told him he didn't understand. It was he who was missing something. I was in great shape. I didn't really need all that. I could skip all that and go straight to the heart of the matter. Looking back, I guess I was asking for the pill that he told me didn't exist.

What I didn't know then was that in Asia, no matter what you do, no matter what kind of physical shape you're in, it doesn't matter when it comes to elevating your spiritual life. Even if you are in martial arts or whatever, you must first show that you have the right stamina, endurance, perseverance, and attitude. Finally, I gave in. If he wanted me to come to exercise classes, I'd go. The second thing he told me was, "I think you Americans use the expression 'check me out.' I want you to follow me. I want you to watch me. And if I'm not exactly everything I'm supposed to be, don't come back." I thought that was pretty cool.

Everything Swamiji did and said came with a deeper meaning. Even the exercise lessons had a lesson beyond the physical exercise. He charged a dollar because he said that if people got it for free they wouldn't appreciate it. Little by little, I began learning. He'd come to the class, and he'd walk around, looking at us, never really paying any attention to me. I could have been a stone until one day, I was told I was going to be initiated into the yogic order. What that means is I was going to receive a mantra. Swamiji was going to give me a special word to use for prayer. That word is geared to you, to your personality. It has special meaning, special energy.

I became a student, a devotee and began to spend a lot of time with Swamiji. I started going to his lectures as well as his exercise classes and I really got to know him. Not only that, but for some unknown reason, he really came to like me. I don't know why, considering how we had first met, but I'm honored that he did. Another high honor, one of which I hold with tremendous pride, is the spiritual name—Paalitha—that Swamiji bestowed upon me. Paalitha, which means "protector," remains a special honor as I would come to realize that for Swamiji, spiritual names were earned through a sincere attempt at true devotion. It's a little like being given a middle name which happens during your confirmation in the Catholic religion. The difference is that you don't choose your "new" name. Swamiji chooses it for you. Another way of looking at it is in terms of how the Pope receives a new name when he is elevated to that height. The idea is to erase your past, the person you were previously, so you can move forward on a new path.

In my desire to introduce Swamiji to everyone I knew, including the Rascals among others—many of whom stuck with him and became extremely devoted students, while some just brushed it off like it was nothing—I got him to come to Hawaii with the Rascals, on what was the most wonderful trip of my life. He came as my guest when we played there. He wasn't alone; accompanying him were his aides, the people who looked after him. Before Swamiji could join us, I was told of a problem in need of being sorted out. Swamiji would like to go, his people told me, but he needed some help, someone there to look after his needs every day. At the top of the list was food because he had a special diet.

The Rascals had an amazing following, including those who found their way to an endless number of shows: groupies, band aides, devotees, enthusiasts, many who we'd get to know better as time rocked on. One, in particular, was Kay Zar. Bands knew her as "Kay Zar, the movie star." When the Beatles first came to California, two friends of hers rented a helicopter and they all dropped into the backyard of the place where the Beatles were staying. The publicity from that stunt got her a write-up in Life Magazine. That's the kind of person she was—the most efficient "Girl Friday" I ever met in my life: an insanely intelligent groupie. To give you an example, most people don't realize that when the big rock stars play places like Madison Square Garden or the Hollywood Bowl, they go in through a special entrance in a limousine. Kay knew that and, if she wanted to meet rock stars, she'd simply rent a limousine and in she'd go, right behind the stars she wanted to meet. She really was creative.

Kay happened to be in the room when I was talking with Swamiji's people. She immediately said, "I'll go. I'll go." I said, "Kay, this is a holy man. What do you know about holy men?" She wouldn't back down. That was Kay. She wanted in on this trip, and so she came with us. We went to the island of Oahu and were treated like royalty. They gave us a private home with a chef and a swimming pool, and they even had a special guest house in the rear of the property where Swamiji stayed. I stayed there, and so did Kay. We had this little three-bedroom "shack," and that's where our own mini "Magical Mystery Tour" really began. It was the most amazing week.

First, we had this holy man there, so the kind of atmosphere where you'd bring girls in and smoke dope, that wasn't going to happen. But it was also a different kind of magic—at least for me. Having so much access to Swamiji was special. It was also a pretty big change for the other Rascals. We had an unbelievable dinner prepared every night by a wonderful Japanese chef, and, after dinner, Swamiji would give us a lecture. It was magical. We could ask him anything we wanted to ask him, which was a rare opportunity as all too often, there'd be too many people around him to gain such an intimate audience with him. I took full advantage of our living arrangement. He was such a great teacher.

Swamiji wasn't always a holy man. He was born into the Brahmin class and was married and had a family at one time. He was in a lot of businesses, including one, believe it or not, which made cars that ran on burning wood. Swamiji wrote his own book in which he talks a lot about how he became the man he was. It all began when his wife died. Amid his grief, he decided to follow the teachings of yoga. He gave up the regular life he had. He was a decent businessman, his family had a farm, he had a good amount of money, and he gave it all up to follow this spiritual path. In some ways, death—his wife's and my mother's—really may be what brought us together, at least at the start. We had a shared experience and faced some of the same questions about the meaning of death—and life.

So here was Swamiji in Hawaii. His housing and diet concerns all worked out. It still must have seemed a little strange to him sitting across the table from four Rascals and a couple of road managers. But it never showed. In fact Swamiji adored young Eddie Brigati. Swamiji was in tune with the fact that Eddie was the furthest thing from a saint in our band. But the rapport that he had with Eddie was magical. Eddie, at that time, had a charming personality with, how shall I say it, raw edges; I'm talking really raw edges. So, when Eddie would talk with Swamiji, even though it sounded like he was a wise guy, he was still being kind of reverent. Swamiji had never experienced somebody like Eddie. To be candid, there aren't many guys like Eddie on the planet.

Swamiji used to call him "the happy monk." That came from one night when Eddie was ready to go out with some girl he'd picked up. "Where are you going, Eddie?" Swamiji asked. Eddie, thinking quickly, said, "Oh, I'm just going out because I gotta teach this girl some exercises." It was as if his date was going to include a yoga session. Swamiji smiled and said, "That's good, Eddie. So, you have some good poses." Eddie, moving quickly out the door, answered: "Oh, I definitely have some good poses." It was a blast. Eddie also used to sing to Swamiji, mimicking the old Al Jolson song, "Swami, how I love ya, how I love ya." I never knew anybody who had Eddie's kind of personality where he loves you, but he's also going to tease you to death. That was Eddie.

Being in Hawaii with Swamiji, my band mates, and my family was just unbelievable. I'm the kind of person who when I get involved in something, I don't just put my foot in the pool. I dive in. I really was overwhelmed by the whole process that Swamiji taught. I became a vegetarian, exercised every day, and engaged in meditation. I still do all that to this day. As I've told my sister, Fran, at my age, it's not really a choice. In order to stay in the kind of good physical and mental health to do all the travel required to tour, I have to do it.

Before I really dove into this lifestyle, however, I checked it out. Remember that Swamiji himself had urged me to ask around, find out everything I could about him, and make sure he was the real deal. Well, I was in England shortly thereafter and met with George Harrison at his home. George's relationship with the Maharishi had already become legendary. But even with that, I needed to ask. I needed to hear it from someone who'd traveled the road, who had begun the journey I had been so seriously contemplating. I asked him, point-blank, if this was for real. George's response couldn't have been more earnest. He said, "Absolutely, Felix. There's absolutely no doubt in my mind." At that point, I felt comfortable that I could jump into this river of faith for the rest of my life.

Over the years, I spent so much time with Swamiji that how I live my daily life has been totally affected by him. The way the yogis see it, you should spend at least twelve years studying with your teacher. The reason they say that is because every twelve years, every cell in your body changes;

every twelve years, your cells are regenerated. The yogis teach that it also takes that long for every cell in your body to be affected by the energy received from your teacher. Twelve is the magic number. I suppose it also shows that you have perseverance since learning what you need to know isn't an overnight process; it takes time.

Throughout my life, Swamiji has been a major presence and influence. He passed away in 2002, having lived nearly 90 years, accomplishing so much, and touching so many people. He's been credited as the founder of integral yoga, he also founded the Yogaville ashram in Virginia, New York, San Francisco, and other places. Most people may not remember this, but he opened the Woodstock festival in 1969, with these words:

I am very happy to see that we are all gathered to create some "making" sounds, to find that peace and joy through the celestial music. I am honored for having been given the opportunity of opening this great, great music festival.

Swamiji was flown in by helicopter to give that blessing. I wish we, the Rascals, had played there, but it wasn't meant to be. As his reputation spread, I wasn't the only devoted follower he had in show business. The actor Jeff Goldblum was another, as was the actress Lauren Hutton, diet expert Dean Ornish, and singer-songwriter Carole King, who also deeded some land she owned to Swamiji for his yogi organization. In the 1970s, he attracted hundreds of thousands of followers. His nutritional ideas were so popular that the Pillsbury corporation even asked for his advice. Swamiji became so eminent that he even appeared at Carnegie Hall.

Yogaville still exists. It's run like a commune. The people who live there are devotees of Swamiji, and they hold retreats. It's self-sufficient. I used to go there a lot more when Swamiji was alive. It's a great place that includes an incredible shrine. It's a symbol of all religions. That was at the center of Swamiji's teachings: that there's really no difference in religions beyond language and the ways you're taught. When you get down to the basics, when you get down to the core, religion, he would say, was about one thing: community. Every religion has its own rules about how its followers connect with God or with a "god." It doesn't matter what you call it, it's still about communing with your fellow human beings on this earth.

So, we met in New York, spent time in Hawaii, and also spent time together on the road. In a way, I even kind of acted like his "road manager" when he toured Europe. He'd do lectures that would sometimes run two or three hours. Anybody who has ever tried to keep an audience's attention for even one hour can attest to how hard that can be, but three hours? Come on. I know Bruce Springsteen can do it every night, but he's got a band! Swamiji just had his words. That's a real challenge. Sometimes, when I think about it, I still can't believe he could have an audience, tens of thousands of people, in the palm of his hand just through the strength of his words. Now, that's powerful.

There was no audience, from Woodstock to Carnegie Hall, that he couldn't mesmerize. When we were in Hawaii, that disc jockey friend who played all our records also recognized the power Swamiji had to grab and keep an audience. One day he was so moved by Swamiji that he invited him to be a guest on his radio show. Swamiji accepted the invitation and took calls from listeners for three or four hours. It was unbelievable. Hawaii had never seen anything like it. After that, the island kind of adopted him, just as they had the Rascals.

I asked him one time whether he planned his talks, whether he had at least an idea of what he was going to speak about before you go out there in front of a crowd?" He thought for a second and replied that he didn't. "Wait a minute. You mean to tell me you go out on stage and don't have anything prepared?"

"That's right," he said with a sly grin. His explanation was that he was completely at the mercy of the people out there listening, and whatever energy they sent out would inspire him to say something. And, of course, they also asked questions. Being an entertainer, naturally, this interested me.

"What if nobody says anything?" I asked.

"Then I go home."

"You're kidding, right?"

"Well, they came to see me, right? So, if they don't want to see anymore of me or ask any questions, I just go home." Wow. No ego. No remorse. He would just go home. Can you imagine? No regret. He just went home. What a lesson for all of us who worry about how others receive what we're saying or, in my case, sing.

That whole way of looking at things changed me. Swamiji's words still connect with me. When I go on stage, I don't worry about anything because I realize they came to see me. That's why they're there. What should I have to worry about? I've never been nervous since that conversation with this wise man. From that day forward I understood, finally, how simple life can be. We make it complicated, but Swamiji kept it simple. How many artists have I sat with backstage, and they say things like "I'm afraid to go out there?" Swamiji's presence appears, his words echoing as I think to myself: "Why would you be afraid? You're good; otherwise, you wouldn't be here and the people in those seats wouldn't have come to hear you." That's one of the important things Swamiji taught me and nobody over here in America is going to teach you that. It comes from the Eastern religions; it's an integral part of their perspective on life, one which is very different from those of us in the Western world.

I learned from Swamiji that a lot of people are really, really misinformed about life. That's where his methods of teaching kicked in. He was not a mystical person; he was very down to earth, kind of mundane, with a talent to fix anything. One story that comes to mind is an instance where two people got up at a meeting of those who had followed Swamiji for a long time. The idea was to tell a story about how you first met Swamiji. Well, they had come all the way from California, and now they were ready for this mystical being to appear in spiritual splendor. It didn't happen that way. Just before they got up to tell their story, they asked where Swamiji was and when they would see him. The person in charge of the meeting told them that Swamiji was out back, covered in motor oil. He'd apparently taken apart a tractor or something. When he came out, Swamiji said, "Excuse me. I had to fix this thing." So, there's your guru—a man just like the rest of us. He's a regular down-to-earth person. That's the man I studied with. The man who helped shape the man I'd become.

The changes the yogi lifestyle brings to your existence are startling. People from outside the rock and roll business have this perception that rock groups are pretty much a bunch of wild animals, totally out of control. They're not wrong. Sometimes, especially back in the days when things were pretty much wide open with sex and drugs, people were completely out of control. By contrast, Yogi was a way of life that, among other things, kept you out of trouble. Following the "prescription"—eating well, meditating, exercising—which is all pretty simple, probably is how I stayed sane in what is really an insane arena.

Swamiji liked to play "word games," messing around with the meaning of a word by picking apart its syllables. Here's an example: disease. Swamiji would say, "You start off with 'ease' and then you 'dis' stroy it." Another he liked to play with was the word "disappointment." He'd grin and say it starts off with an appointment that you have, but then, when you don't show up, it becomes a "dis" appointment because your absence was a "dis" to the other person. Stuff like that really amused him. He was really someone right down here, right on your level, not way above in some mystical place that no one could ever even hope to visit, let alone reach.

In many ways, I think everybody I knew at the time was surprised, maybe shocked is a better word, because I was engaging in something that was pretty much the opposite of a rock and roll lifestyle. I think the Rascals, especially, really thought I'd lost my mind. I dressed all in white. I was a vegetarian. I didn't smoke. I didn't drink. To be honest, the only thing I really had trouble eliminating was sex. When you get it down to once a month, for a rocker like me, you're doing pretty well. I used to resist temptation by staying in a different part of the hotel from the others so I could avoid giving in. In those days, it was pretty wild. It wasn't easy. But I really tried to live by his tenets. I really tried. It was kind of like being a monk.

I had women in my life, of course, and that was okay, said Swamiji, "But Felix, you've got to stop fooling around." Keep in mind: there's no fooling around in yoga. If you were married or you were committed to a woman, that was fine, he would say, but you can't be running around with multiple women. That's not okay, according to his teachings, which it really isn't in most, if not all, religions. That, too, wasn't different from the moral path a lot of people try to follow, but it just made so much more sense to me coming from such a man.

I can only add that I was really, really blessed to spend time with a man of his caliber. He helped me in so many ways. If I were to sum it all up in one word, it would probably be "karma." There are a lot of definitions of the word, but the story I tell that I think best illustrates its meaning starts with asking an Indian for directions. A half an hour later, you're still listening because he still hasn't gotten to the point. An Indian would tell the story somewhat like this: "First you go there, then you see that, and then watch for the other." You want to say, "Come on, do I turn yet? When will I get to where I'm going?" Well, in yogi, the story is the whole point. It's about focusing on your inner space, not, as in Western thinking, the space outside you.

It's like retraining yourself to do the best you can and let the rest fall into place. Most of us let the monetary side of our lives take over. Swamiji taught me to stay on the spiritual side of my existence. Here's another simple story that I always remember. One day, frustrated with how things were going, I said to him something along the lines of "Don't you ever think about how we need to change the world?"

His response was, "Felix, I gave you a broom and told you to clean out your closet. Now you want to clean up the whole house. You can't clean up the world until you clean up yourself." That, too, is karma. That kind of logic spoke to me and helped get my life more closely in balance.

There was even a time when I thought I might enter the world of yoga full-time, but, as I've already admitted, there were certain pleasures I couldn't see myself giving up entirely. From our conversations, it was also obvious to me that Swamiji felt there was a different purpose to my life. It was funny because, while he was around rock and roll people all the time, the Rascals included, he didn't embrace that form of music. In fact, he didn't even allow rock and roll to be played around him or his followers at the ashram, however, he made an exception for Rascals records, and I've always been touched by that. Albums like "Peaceful World" and "Island of Real," and especially the songs "Beautiful Morning" and "Groovin," were the only rock records he would allow to be played in his ashram. I think what he really liked and approved of was the way the audience absorbed the energy of our music.

That tied into how he experienced our shows; from up close, he was an observer, not just of us, but of the crowd. In addition to all his other attributes—holy man, teacher, do-it-yourselfer, inventor— Swamiji was a photographer and a really good one. I can see it now in my mind: Swamiji at our shows, taking shots of us on stage, but, even more so, of those in the audience. After one show, Swamiji said to me, "You know, what you do is really important. YOU are really important to these kids." That not only made me feel good, but it also guided the direction of my life. Music could bring joy. Music was part of karma. It could lift us up and ennoble us. It was my "broom" as Swamiji had previously described. I'd always found joy in playing with the Rascals, but I was starting to see that joy came from within. Swamiji had helped to enlighten the 13-year-old kid inside me.

Who knows where inspiration comes from? Looking back, there was a song I wrote in 1969 called "See." It shows where I was in terms of my music and songwriting at that time and it wasn't even close to where the others in the band were or would be. It was a LONG way from "Good Lovin'," both musically and lyrically. It really reflected my yogi roots more than my Rascals roots and that became a problem. While they were around Swamiji sometimes, especially in Hawaii, the other Rascals were never really into that whole scene, and as I've suggested, they sometimes thought I'd lost my mind entirely. It was interesting to see how people perceive you differently when you're not part of *their* scene. When I started separating myself from the others—from the alcohol, drugs, and sex all around us in those days—it had an immediate, and lasting impact on the band. The problem with being around people who drink and drug when you don't is that they really don't *want* you around. For one thing, with time and age, I've figured out that they don't want you looking down on them, but they sure as hell don't want to be looking up at you.

Chapter 7: Paying it Forward

Discrimination on any level is a hard pill to swallow, no matter how intensely it's struck upon you. Pelham was a wasp town that had been very keen on keeping that way. The disrespect shown to my mother by the Flower Club was hard to witness, as was my dad's response to his rejection from membership into the country club. These were my parents, and they were being discriminated against solely due to the roots of their blood. The pain I felt on their behalf may very well have been more intense than any pain they may have felt, but it hurt, and the pain stuck. Still does.

There were other reasons behind my rejection of prejudice and bigotry—toward anybody, anywhere—and they also go back to my youth. Our parents did everything to give us the great upbringing we had in Pelham, but there was always some kind of racial profiling that I noticed. If you were Italian, you felt it. If you were Spanish, you felt it. You could see that minorities were being treated differently from everybody else and that always had an effect on me. It really hit home when a kid from my high school, Micky Schwerner, was killed in Mississippi in 1964. It was a very famous event. He was a Jewish kid who had gone down there with the Freedom Summer Campaign trying to register African Americans in Mississippi to vote. He and two other young people lost their lives and that really had an impact on my thinking. They made a movie called

"Mississippi Burning" that's loosely based on what happened to Micky and the others. I've never forgotten that a kid from *our neighborhood* had his life taken away just for trying to do the right thing.

As a kid, I'd strangely force myself into untenable situations just to see how I would get out of them. One such situation would be purposely walking until I didn't know where I was and then try to find my way back home. Well, one afternoon, I found myself truly lost. The sun was going down, and it was clear that I had no idea where the hell I was. But I did find myself in a nice neighborhood. It was almost dark, and I was scared, my eyes welling, I finally got the nerve to knock on a door. A pleasant yet cautious woman answered the door. "Excuse me, ma'am I'm trying to get home. Can you help me?" Not only wouldn't she help, she shut the door in my face.

As dusk was settling in, the maids from these homes were leaving and going back to their families. A lovely black woman came up and asked if I was ok. I wasn't, and she could see it. She asked where I lived. "592 Colonial Avenue." She put me in her husband's car and drove me right to my front door. It's a memory that has held up so well within my mind: her smile, her hair, her smell, her eyes, and her skin. This complete stranger did more than touch my soul. She held it in her hands. To this day, when I feel that I'm in danger, I look to a brother or sister to help me out.

Race has never mattered to me. We're all just people. I was listening to a lot of black music as a kid because that's what rock and roll was. It was either black musicians, or white musicians trying to sound black. Folk music also began speaking to me. Songs by Peter Paul and Mary, Pete Seegar, and Sam Cooke, among others, began to create an attitude that "Change was gonna come." It had to, it was time, there was no more looking the other way and I feel blessed to have been a part of it.

I remember one day, while working in the Catskills, one of the ladies working, heard me in the lounge rehearsing. She came up to me and said, "Son, you are sanctified! God is within you, believe me." I felt the connection, always have.

The music within me is the most tangible effect, but the overwhelming feeling that we are all created equal has stuck. If we analyze music, we see that in classical music, most of the rhythms are either Timpani, for dramatic effect, or war-like marching rhythms, drums, perhaps some thunder and lightning sounds. Whereas in India, Africa, and the Middle East, dancing and captivating rhythms dominate. It's putting the two together that has brought us modern music. Pretty simple formula isn't it!

In the south in the '60s and '70s, many music venues were segregated. When we played there, we had to be really careful. Remember, we had long hair, and down south, that didn't really go over too well with some people. One time we ran out of gas driving back from a show and had to make an emergency stop and I thought we were going to get killed by the locals. It was a very different world, one that this bunch of kids from New York wasn't exactly used to if you know what I mean. Because I'd always played in "mixed" groups, I never really got the idea that, when it came to playing some places, the audiences were all white and no one, I mean *no one* else who played on the bill was black. As soon as we could, I vowed to change that.

The Rascals always crossed over, which made me proud. Being the first white group signed to Atlantic Records gave us tremendous pride. Black radio stations played us from the very beginning. We made music for everyone. We were a crossover band, before the term "crossover was ever created.

Each of us in the Rascals had experience playing with black musicians and felt like we probably shared a thread with them in the discrimination department. When he was only 15, Dino, for example, played with jazz legend Lionel Hampton. I've already detailed how the earliest groups I formed in both high school and at Syracuse University always involved black and white players and Joey Dee always had mixed bands. Rhythm and Blues was where my inspiration came from, and I always felt the urgency to pay that forward. Here we were borrowing so much from black music, but they couldn't come to hear us play what was essentially *their* music. That pissed us off.

It was this continued education that further formulated our social consciousness to the point where I felt it was imperative that we do our part in the movement toward social justice for all, and what better way than through music? The radio stations at that time played a mix of music. It wasn't white music or black music. It was just music. When we'd be driving through some of these southern towns, I was constantly exposed as a young man to songs I'd never heard before. On one occasion, I remember hearing a song called "Mockingbird." It was by Inez and Charlie Foxx and recorded in 1963. It blew me away. I was like, "Stop the car. Stop the car. I have to listen to this." I sat there in an almost meditative state and allowed the song to penetrate every part of my mind. That's how deeply soul music affected me.

I knew that black artists weren't getting the recognition they deserved, everything from their fair share of record royalties to the limited opportunities to play before bigger audiences due to segregation. Think about all the great music that wasn't being heard. The fact that black artists had such a limited platform in reaching broader audiences wasn't right.

This wasn't a new revelation for me. I'd seen it before, going back to my childhood, but also while at Syracuse University. I always believed it was important to stand up against discrimination and segregation. College brought my first, full-on experience with segregation. Being in a fraternity, I played at most of our parties. Figuring I could have some influence on my fellow frat brothers, I really tried to get some of the African Americans to pledge. I figured I could change the world. Go figure. My intentions were good, but after trying a few times, a few of the guys came up to me and said, "Felix, we love you, and we appreciate what you're trying to do, but you're going to get us killed, brother."

Once I got in a position of having some kind of influence, I decided to take a stand. We started to put in our contracts that anywhere we played, there had to be a black act on the bill with us. A huge problem for a lot of music promoters in some parts of the country was the fear of alienating their white audiences. We insisted, held firm, and refused to play within the concept of segregation.

Groups like "The Friends of Distinction" have said they never played in front of a white audience before opening for us on tour. It's the same with another black group, "Young Holt Unlimited," who had a hit with a song titled "Soulful Strut." It was good to hear that we helped clear some kind of path for our fellow artists. But the truth is that despite the fact it cost us a lot of money, hundreds of thousands if not millions, with promoters in some parts of the country refusing to book us, it was the right thing to do. It was quite simply my way of saying thank you!

It's not like it was something I consciously started out to do. I'm a musician, not a politician. On the other hand, so many social changes occurred in the '60s that I was there to see and experience first-hand. Like others of my generation, I remember when the Peace Corps was started by President Kennedy. I saw the moon-landing, participated in the Civil Rights movement, and supported voter rights. There were marches, protests, the Vietnam War. We, as musicians, were right in the middle of it all. I think in one way or another, the songs Eddie and I wrote reflect those times. They each have universal themes of love, happiness, gratitude, and serenity. There's nothing negative about "It's a Beautiful Morning" or "Groovin'." They're both celebrations of life. Even "Lonely Too Long" reflects everyone's need to, as the lyric goes, "find someone."

They're also filled with hope, which is something I think was inspired by President Kennedy. All things seemed possible.

In many ways, "People Got to Be Free" was what changed the musical landscape for me and for the Rascals. I've already discussed how it was written, but I think it's important to say that it really expressed what was burning inside of me, what made me want to fight discrimination everywhere, in every place, and in every form. It originated while I was working for the Robert Kennedy campaign. First, there was Martin Luther King's death, and then Bobby Kennedy's assassination. It was almost crippling. I had been dating a young lady who got me involved with the Kennedy family, and she was actually with Bobby Kennedy when he was assassinated. Right there, just a few feet from him as he was shot. Something clicked that day. A voice screaming inside my head telling me, "You're here for a reason." It was, I think, something inside of me that just had to get out. I had to make a statement and that statement, in a lot of ways, ended up being what drove the Rascals' stand on social justice and civil rights. "People Got to Be Free" was less a song than a calling, an exclamation. A sentimentality that exploded out of me with a sense of emotion so forceful that more often than not, it still grips me while performing it on stage.

When it came to taking a stand, the Rascals were also in good company, though I can't say I knew it at the time. Another Italian gentleman named Frank Sinatra had taken a similar stand against prejudice in 1964. Even going back to the Joey Dee days, while we'd all play together on stage, after the show, the black musicians had to go back to stay in a different hotel from where we stayed. The same thing happened to the musicians who played with Sinatra at the Sands Hotel in Las Vegas. Sinatra finally had enough when he was told members of Count Basie's band couldn't stay at the Sands. He made it clear that this was going to change. Quincy Jones, who was at that time a member of the Basie band, remembers that Sinatra insisted they all would be given rooms right there at the Sands, not at the "black hotel" down the street. He said that if anyone tried to interfere or even looked funny at the band, he'd see that their legs were broken. That was pretty powerful.

That's the way it was. It was part of the whole fabric of the '60s. People were either for the war or against it. There were mods or rockers, preppies or hippies. A lot of anxiety; a ton of intensity. We ran into a lot of problems once we took our stand that all Rascals shows had to have a black act playing with us. I remember one show where the Black Panthers came out and protested. I met Stokley Carmichael, one of the group's leaders. He said, "I got no problem with you, but we got problems with the people who are putting on the show." I said, "No problem, do what you gotta do." We, as a band decided not to play that night.

I've had the great fortune to meet many of the civil rights giants over the years. Bobby Kennedy, John Lewis, Elijah Cummings, and Dick Gregory just to name a few. ASCAP sent me on lobbying trips to DC to promote our publishing and songwriting rights which provided me with further opportunity to "whisper in their ears." As did the concerts I had the pleasure of playing at the Library of Congress that were attended by many members of the House and Senate, which also provided me the opportunity to see the vaults of the library where many original manuscripts of Beethoven, Mozart, Chopin are preserved along with so many more. I'm proud to say that "People Got to Be Free" is in there as well. A true thrill!

So many people, as well as organizations like the Panthers were fighting for their rights. And I have to admit I was pretty radical in my own ideas in those days and, in a lot of ways, I still I am, especially for someone living where I now make my home, in the south. It's very different from the east or the west coasts. Politically, I'm such a minority, it's just ridiculous. As part of my 60's mentality, I really haven't changed. I think I may have gotten worse. The same kind of stuff that bothered me then still bothers me now. What's more important, the country's well-being or your self-interests? Is it about everybody or just your own pocketbook?

Yes, I've been very fortunate, and I remain supremely thankful. But it's 2022 AND WE STILL DON'T GET IT.

Chapter 8: The Rascals Breakup

If 1967 was the summer of love, 1969 was the morning after. I've always found the beauty in life and songs inspired by beauty, by love, by optimism, by magic, and by the possibility of it all. In 1969 I had to search deeper to find the beauty. It was there, I just had to delve deeper to find it.

As a band, our rock and soul influences of the mid-60s had evolved. Our music, our world and our influences had all come of age. Once again, the times, like always, were a changin'. Time threatens to pass us all by. The choice is in whether we smile and wave with a soulful ping or stubbornly attach ourselves to the bitterness of labeling yesterday an adversary of tomorrow.

1969 was the beginning of the end of us as a band. Remember that we had an album called "Once Upon a Dream" the previous year and that's really what our life together, up to that point, had been: pretty much a dream come true. Well, the nightmare was about to begin. It's funny how everyone who is part of any experience sees it differently from the others who were there at the time; that's another way of saying that each of the other three Rascals may tell the story differently, but that's up to them. They can write their own books, but in this book, I can only tell you the way I see our breakup and it may not be pretty, but it is the truth, as I know it.

Everybody can have his opinion, but the facts are the facts.

Eddie had quit the band for a brief period right after we recorded "People Got to be Free" for the "Freedom Suite" album about a year before. We had seen less and less of him in the studio, and his input and contributions began to diminish until he pretty much became non-existent in his writing and singing. When he did make it into the studio, he'd sing his part then get the hell out. He wanted no part of the process of recording, mixing, arrangements, basically any studio work.

There were a lot of drugs around during this time. And, in my opinion, Eddie was becoming a bit paranoid, his actions and mood swings growing evermore intense. It was like a Jekyll and Hyde thing. One minute he was totally cool, full of energy, high on life, and the next minute he'd be pissed off at the world and everyone around him, followed suddenly by sad Eddie walking around with a cloud hanging over him, all of his energy extinguished.

We had a problem, a big problem, so we put together a meeting of all four of us, together with Swami, at his place, along with our lawyer and our manager. At this meeting, I realized that the problems were even bigger than I could have imagined. Every other word out of Eddie's mouth had to do with "fear," or every sentence had fear in it. It was like he thought everybody was out to get him. That meeting ended up with Swami telling him, "Eddie, I want to tell you something. You've been given a gift. The people adore you. You have to share that gift. That's why you're here on this planet. You're not here to go home and make wood carvings. You're here to share your gift." I remember Swami's words bringing tears to Eddie's eyes. So, for a while, Eddie came back to the group. It was actually the meeting with Swamiji that may have convinced him not to quit.

The reality is that Eddie came back in name only. Getting him into the studio was like pulling teeth; he showed no excitement or enthusiasm for the work. It would have been one thing if he communicated his need for some time off, 'like hey, I really need a vacation,' or something like that, but he was positively vehement whenever anyone questioned him, always in attack mode. He was combative about almost everything, starting with the contention that one line in any song is worth 50% of the writing credit. Frankly, that's just not the way songwriters do things, sure 50% music, 50% lyrics… but not just one line.

One day he came into the situation with his guns at the ready as if he had enemies behind every corner. I tried to point out that one line in a song doesn't equal 50%, meaning that, going forward, I needed him in the studio, co-writing lyrics and putting in the effort. In other words, I told him that he needed to get to work. Unfortunately, he wasn't hearing it. We had one more album on our Atlantic contract and we were falling further and further behind. All of this affected the music, and it affected the lyrics. It affected the whole vibe.

As great a visionary as Sid Bernstein was, he was less a manager and more a babysitter. A guy that yessed us to death, he wasn't the type of hands-on manager who would drive the band; it just wasn't his style. He was too soft, and Eddie would treat him and our lawyer as if they were idiots and crooks. I mean, here's our lawyer, Steven Weiss, another industry legend, listing Led Zeppelin, Jimi Hendrix, Vanilla Fudge among just a few of his clients, and here he was being constantly berated by Eddie. It was insane. Sid began communicating solely with me, even with Eddie in the room, while Steve just stopped attending our meetings altogether. And that, like everything else, set Eddie off.

The band and our music were the only things in my life at that time that completely consumed me. That's it. Not relationships with women, not partying, nothing. I was a 'studio-rat' forced to do more and more of the writing, producing, and singing. Did I want Eddie there? Hell yes! I wanted his writing input, and I wanted his voice. I missed not having him in the studio. I missed the Eddie who would sprinkle flowers upon the songs I created.

While I was in the studio working on our last album with Atlantic, "Search and Nearness," Sid Bernstein and Steven Weiss were in the midst of negotiations with Atlantic to renew our contract. My preference was to stay with Atlantic, to keep our team together and to continue recording with Arif, but I was told that Atlantic had no intention of re-signing the Rascals, but that Jerry Wexler did, however, want to sign a new deal with me. I didn't want to leave Atlantic, but the only way I'd stay was to sign a new contract as a Rascal, not as a solo artist. I asked that Sid begin to seek out a new label for us—not me—but for us, as in The Rascals. Our last albums with Atlantic were good musically, but they didn't have the commercial success of our earlier work and didn't produce monster singles like "Good Lovin'" and "Groovin'." They were a little less accessible, not so radio-friendly as those songs and the others that had kept us on the charts.

Record companies are only happy when they make money. No money, no happiness. We'd been pretty much a "corporation"—that's really what a band is when you get that successful, but now the corporation was having problems and that caused problems for the record executives—and, with that, our relationship with Atlantic became a thing of the past.

The problem was we still had an album to finish, "Search & Nearness," but with Eddie so far removed, we were forced to bring in other artists from the Atlantic label to sing and it no longer felt like the Rascals, but we had to finish the album; we owed it to the label. At this point, it became tough. It had become more like an obligation than a creation. On top of it all, we knew Atlantic wasn't going to promote the album. Why would they? We were leaving the label.

It was at this time that David Geffen approached me to produce an album for his client, Laura Nyro. He had stated that both he and Laura were fans and that she'd love the opportunity to work with me. Laura, a fellow New Yorker, was a brilliant singer and songwriter who penned such iconic hits as "Wedding Bell Blues" and "Stoned Soul Picnic" for the 5th Dimension, as well as "And When I Die" for Blood Sweat & Tears. Laura was under contract with Columbia Records at the time and Geffen warned me that I was about to meet the most difficult person I'd ever known.

The album was called "Christmas and the Beads of Sweat." I brought in Arif Mardin from Atlantic as co-producer. I've talked a lot about Arif's many talents and among them was his ability to leave his ego behind and allow himself to feel the talent in others. It didn't take much to convince Arif to join me in producing Laura's album. Nor did it take long for Laura to adore Arif as much as I did. The relationship between Arif and I was so strong that eventually we formed our own production company, Mevlana, named after a Turkish Saint, which Arif certainly was.

Laura was without question as pure and uncompromising an artist as I've ever come across. She was the total perfectionist. I tend to hesitate when using the word brilliant, but never with Laura. She had absolute zero concern with anything commercial. She had the sound of her songs so firmly implanted within her mind that it took a bulldozer to even allow her to become open to anyone's input. Working with Laura and producing with Arif was a wonderful experience and one I looked forward to repeating for years to come; however, that wasn't to be the case. Atlantic Records was too hip and too smart to let Arif go. They offered him the position of Vice President along with a salary that made him a rich man and although it hurt professionally, personally I couldn't have been happier for him. Arif was finally going to get the reward and recognition from Atlantic that he deserved.

It was right about this time that Columbia Records presented us with a four album, $2,000,000 deal. Plus, Columbia was an international company, where Atlantic really wasn't at that time, in the years before they were acquired by Warner. It would be a big move forward for the Rascals, or at least what remained of us. It would put us on the global map.

I felt that Columbia shared my belief that the passion is the music, that it's the quest for inspiration, the love of the instrument and the soulful search of the voice that breeds great music. I didn't believe they were into analyzing market trends or steeping the tea leaves in the hopes of rendering a crystal ball that would reveal the "hits" of tomorrow.

The Rascals had several big songs of our time because we were of that time, but like me, Columbia had its eye on the future. They weren't looking for remakes of yesterday's greatest hits. And while signing with Columbia would provide us with the ability to tap into many of their amazing musicians, my hope was for the four of us to remain a band. However, it wasn't meant to be. I really wasn't seeking to be a "Felix." I wanted to continue to be a "Rascal."

The four of us, Eddie, Dino, Gene, and I, arrived at the contract signing with Sid Bernstein and Steven Weiss. There was a ton of great energy. We were excited. Columbia and their representatives were excited. There was a great feeling in the air. The contract was right there on the table in front of us. I turned to the band and attempted a bit of a pep talk, you know, to get us rallied. "This is a great opportunity for us." I told them, "There's a lot of money and a lot of work on the table. Let's do this, okay?"

We went around the room. Gene said, "Oh man, this is what I dreamed about my entire life. This is going to be great." Dino, a professional who showed up for work every day, was more abrupt, saying, "Come on, of course I want to do this. Let's go." Next, it was Eddie's turn, and he started going around the room, literally attacking everyone. He started with Sid, saying, "You don't give a shit about us." Then to our lawyer, Steven Weiss, he blared out "You have no integrity, you're too greedy to care." Then he unleashed on Gene and Dino, and next, I remember him locking in on me, saying that I was an insane workaholic with no regard for anyone's personal time. Hell man, I would have been happy to have Eddie in the studio three days a week, but there he was giving us one day, and there he was yelling at me as if I were asking for seven days a week. He wasn't making any sense, just berating the crap out of all of us. Here we were, contracts right in front of us, a moment in time that called for celebration, but it seemed that Eddie was just too far gone—with paranoia and who knows what else— he simply didn't care about anyone. He just threw a grenade across the room and walked out. We were all in shock.

The tone of the entire room went from celebratory to severely stunned in a matter of minutes. Steven Weiss ran out of the room after Eddie while lawyers for Columbia got on the phone with Clive Davis,

Columbia's president. Steve came back without Eddie and told us he was gone and added that he wasn't coming back. Clive told his people that he didn't give a damn, in his words "That didn't change a thing." The same deal remained on the table and the three of us signed the contract.

I recall preparing to sign on the dotted line and thinking that it wasn't a pen I held in my hand that afternoon but the dream of a lifetime. At twenty-seven years old, that pen was a magic wand that would allow me to live my dream for my lifetime. My love for music and performance was so profound that all I wanted to do at that moment was get my ass into the studio and produce.

Next thing you know, we're on our way to the Bahamas heading for a large music convention where Columbia wanted to celebrate the signing of the Rascals. There we were, just the three of us—me, Gene, and Dino—at what Columbia was considering the roll out of our new association with them. Of course, we still had a "personnel problem." We had to find "another" Eddie, someone to take his place in the group, so we had a "fill-in," a singer named Bruce Bruno, who had a hit single called "Hey, Little One."

When Eddie left the band, he didn't leave to start a new band or to begin a new entity. He just went home. He simply departed. There were so many seeds of discontent along the way, although not all of them had to do with Eddie, but, as I see it, a lot of them did. Honestly, it's my opinion that most of them did. Gene and Dino weren't in a good place either. Slowly but surely, we were falling apart as a band and there didn't seem to be anything any of us could do about it.

Just as we began preparing for the Columbia recording sessions, Dino decided it was time to raise another issue. Now, remember, Dino is undeniably a fantastic drummer, truly a legend in his time, but he's also a very strange guy. One day, he came up with this surprise. "Felix, Eddie's gone, so how about we get rid of Gene?" I was like…what? His whole point seemed to be that we should dump Gene because he really wasn't, in Dino's view, playing anymore.

Dino told me he didn't feel as if Gene was fulfilling his role as our guitarist. I remember saying to Dino, "Come on, man, he's part of the family. What do you mean?" What he meant was that Gene really had backed off on his contributions to the Rascals, spending more time being a "celebrity" than a musician. I could see that, too, but come on, kick the guy out? I wasn't in favor of doing something so severe. It didn't seem right to me, and I don't think it would have been right, given all that the four of us had been through together.

Gene was talented, let there be no mistake about that. The problem was getting him into the studio because at twenty-five and the world at his feet, he was busy buying a Rolls Royce, going out with models, owning horses, whatever fit the image of the celebrity that he thought he'd become.

Gene got caught up in being a "Rock Star," and while his love of performance never waned, his actual performance had. He really got caught up in that, as well as other stuff that kind of went with the territory back then.

Truthfully, nobody in the group loved to play music more than Gene, but he just wasn't playing well, and Dino noticed it. He was right. I recall more than once having Gene ask us to cancel a show because he'd had his eye on a woman for weeks, and "tonight was the night." It was unbelievable. Dino reminded me that since I was the leader of the group, I was responsible for telling Gene that he had to go. And, not unexpectedly, Gene didn't take it well. He was devastated, absolutely devastated, and I knew he would be. There was no surprise there. Who wants to be shown the gate?

We brought in a phenomenal guitar player named Buzzy Feiten, who joined us on the Columbia sessions, yet I started to feel pretty much alone in the studio. Here I was with no Arif around, as in the Atlantic days. I'm in the studio trying to make a lot of things work. I'm completely in charge. If I have a musical question, there's no one around to ask for advice. Like I said, I had to produce the songs, play the songs, and sing the songs.

At least there were some excellent musicians around, like a great bass player named Robert Poparell, but overall, it was just me and Dino and whatever musicians Columbia allowed us to bring in. At one point, I wanted to start over, do a kind of "New Rascals," but Dino, at that point, wasn't in. The irony about all this is that, basically behind my back, Dino started a band with Gene in 1972, called "Bulldog." I think to this day Gene blames me for his troubles back then and I can see his point, but my only goal was to keep the band going. Keep the music alive. I did what I could, and I wasn't perfect.

What hurt the most was seeing the ultimate dissolution of the band. There's nothing better than being a part of a group, especially one like the Rascals that had so much success. And there's nothing worse than when it all just comes apart—especially when there was no real reason for that to happen. It was just stupid. There's no other word for it, but stupid. We literally imploded. We had everything going for us and we should have been smart enough to take advantage of the position we were in. Instead, we argued over stuff that should have been easy. There were so many great opportunities being offered that I wanted to jump on, but the other guys didn't.

It was beyond frustrating for me as well as Sid. As our manager he did everything he could to keep us together, but in the end, he couldn't control us. He was like the father of a bunch of kids who just wouldn't listen. They just wanted everything their own way and there was no longer a lot that we all had in common.

That still seems weird to me. We started out together, got so far, so fast, that I didn't get a chance to slow down a minute and say to myself, what do you really have in common with these guys? I just assumed we all had the same values. But now I knew we didn't. Some of it had to do with our upbringing; we were raised very differently from each other. Eddie, for one, had a rough upbringing. He was raised above a pool hall, his family focused on their next dollar. Whereas I grew up in an environment focused on higher learning.

To this day, with my own children and grandchildren, there's nothing more important. I became especially self-aware of the difference between having an education and not having an education during that first summer after I left Syracuse University. Some of the guys I knew while I was a student there were home and I ran into them. I noticed both a difference and a distance between them and me. "What's happened to you, man?" I remember one of them saying. They were talking about stuff that I had no idea about and even their vocabulary was on a higher level. I've always wanted to be better, be more educated, learn more, do more, go further. That's why, to this day, I read constantly, about every subject you can imagine.

That wasn't the case for the other Rascals, and I'd finally begun to realize that. Eddie was really influenced by his family in a different way than I had been. He really distrusted people. We had all these accountants who handled all the money, but Eddie was convinced the money was being stolen from him. It was bizarre.

Look, did we lose money? Of course, we lost money, but I can't say we were robbed. Everybody in the music business finds out at some point that there's money "missing." It's the business. "Grow up," as Sam and Dave had told me. You have to grow up. But it never seemed like Eddie ever did. He just kept on believing everybody was out to steal from him— the accountants, the managers, the promoters, and, ultimately, me.

What can you say about a young man who was a great little singer and dancer, blessed with all the talent in the world as a lyricist, but still had very few goals in life? I remember one of his goals was to be a funeral director. Wow, a funeral director. When I asked him about that once, he said that, as a child, he wanted to go into the funeral business to ensure that his parents were embalmed correctly. Who thinks that way? In my personal experience, Eddie Brigati, that's who. I also remember Eddie had a big fascination with Harpo Marx. Sometimes he'd ride around on a motorcycle wearing a wig, with one of those bicycle horns that honks. Instead of talking to you, he'd honk the horn the way Harpo did. I never really figured that out, either.

As long as I knew Eddie, I never really felt like I got close to him, despite all those great songs we wrote together. He was of a very different breed. I remember a show we did in Paris. It was an international event, with musicians from all over the world playing—not just from France, but also from Spain, England, Africa. We were America's band in that show, representing the United States. Well, the people who promoted and produced it had trouble finding a Hammond B-3 organ, the instrument I play. Finally, they found one, but a stagehand plugged it into the wrong input and it blew up!

The promoters wanted me to play a different instrument—something called a farfisa—which is like a mini-keyboard, but I refused. It's a poor substitute for the mighty B-3 Hammond. "I can't go on," I told them. "I'm not going to embarrass myself." This went on for a long time, the back and forth, the arguments. Meantime, Eddie is getting more and more nervous. He used to spend a lot of time figuring out what he wanted to wear; he liked the idea of wearing different costumes on stage. That night he was pacing around backstage picking out his costume for the occasion.

Well, finally, I got talked into going out and playing. We went on.

The next thing I know, when we come off stage and Eddie is cursing everybody, me especially. Here he is, the show is over, and we should be relaxing, but my recollection is of Eddie cursing. I'll put it delicately. That costume he finally decided on for his stage appearance? It lasted through our act, but it didn't make it to the rest room. The whole episode of arguing about the musical instrument arrangement had caused Eddie to have an unscheduled pit stop, without the benefit of a pit. The tension backstage apparently brought it on. He didn't handle that situation well.

All this was going on just as the Rascals were being offered several amazing opportunities. For one, we were offered a tour of Japan. Obviously, I wanted to go. There were millions of people in Japan, all wanting to see and hear us play. The others didn't see it that way. It started with Eddie not wanting to go, but eventually I was outvoted by all three of the other Rascals. That was a shame. An even bigger shame was that we were offered a Broadway show. It was a rock opera, long before "Jesus Christ Superstar" came along. A big Broadway producer, David Green, wanted us to do it. We didn't even audition because, once again, there was resistance. "What are you, crazy?" I said to the band. Eddie, for one, thought at the time that we were already working too hard, so we just let the opportunity pass us by. "Don't we work enough already?" were his words, as I remember them.

I once ran into Hal David, who was the songwriting partner of Burt Bacharach. Hal wrote the lyrics and Bacharach wrote the music. They had a ton of monster hits: "Walk On By," "Look of Love," "Raindrops Keep Falling on My Head," "Close to You," the list goes on and on. Well, that night, while at the Rock and Roll Hall of Fame in 1997 when the Rascals were inducted, Hal

David had been talking with Eddie. I don't know what they were talking about, but I know that when the conversation was over, Hal came over to me and said, "You know, Felix, I used to think I had a difficult partner…"

It sounds funny, I know, but the serious part is that Eddie and I started to see less and less of each other and a lot more of our lawyers. The same goes for the other two guys, Gene and Dino. Speaking about an education, I certainly got one in dealing with lawyers. Seriously, I learned a lot about legal matters, and I guess that's a good thing, considering how much the lessons cost me, really cost all of us.

To this day, it has always seemed to me abnormal for a band to sue the creator of the band. But look, a lot of bands go through it. Think about the Beatles, the Beach Boys; it happened to them over some of the same things: money, jealousy, and, of course, you can't discount the influence drugs might have played at the time. I don't know about today, but I doubt it's changed much. People who aren't in their right minds don't generally make good decisions and all I can say is that some of that played into the bad decisions we made—that, plus we had businesspeople who were paid to make those decisions for us and we should have listened to them. They weren't always right, but they were always paid, so why not listen to someone you're paying? Instead, the other guys wanted to just believe they were getting cut out of stuff they were entitled to get. And, somehow, in their minds, I was a part of it.

It's sad. We had everything. I mean everything. Being a musician isn't exactly the toughest job on earth. For those of us who have the privilege of making music for a living, it's really a joy, so why be bitter or worry about what you could have, did have, or lost? It's one of the reasons I like seeing my friend Tommy James when we run into each other on the road. This is a guy who was robbed, and I mean robbed. But he has no bitterness about it. He's just happy people still know his name after all this time and come out to see him.

The other Rascals should feel the same way, in my opinion. By the grace of God, our music was and still is good. Yet, we did everything humanly possible wrong. We did everything we could to screw things up, but the music; the music was good. That's why people still play and listen to it. One of my best friends from the old days, Tommy Calagna, was there with us when we were growing up and progressing in the music business. Tommy is a very astute businessman and I respect his opinion. He also knows the true story of the Rascals, so much so that he put what happened to us—the breakup, the lawsuits, and the bitterness—in a very succinct phrase. We are, Tommy says, "The dumbest rock and roll band in the world."

Why did all this stupidity happen? It's very simple to me; it's called ego. I've been very consistent in how I view the situation. You don't have to read it in this book. You can read it in any one of the hundreds of interviews I've done over the years and ones that I do to this day. I always say the same thing. Nobody took anybody's wife. Nobody committed any embezzlement. No one took any money that didn't belong to them. There was no concrete reason for anyone in this organization to do what we did to each other. To be perfectly honest with you, the only thing I can come up with is Ego, which I purposely spell with a capital "E."

If I could go back, I wouldn't change anything about being with the Rascals, except for perhaps the role that Ego played. As a group, we needed to act more like a group, not just a bunch of individuals looking out only for themselves. When you're with a group, it's really a whole lot of fun. And when you're working, you're working. But when you're with a bunch of guys, I guess it's a lot like what happens with sports teams. You need to act like a unit. There's a camaraderie there that you need in order to win and that means you must have each other's backs.

Even given all the trouble that we had, I still loved being part of a group. There's a lot more "group energy" than "solo energy." A lot of performers who are solo artists, generally speaking, are not "sharers." They're more like "me, me, me." They're not really what I'd call "communal" people, but maybe that's what makes them successful. It's possibly what propels them to such heights. It's almost selfishness. I hate to say it, but I think it is. I really like playing music with other people and I really loved playing music with my original bandmates.

The Rascals went our own way. We began our own lives, minus each other. That doesn't mean there are no social interactions between the Cavalieres and the Brigatis. It's really interesting that our families still co-mingle. One of my daughters is still really good friends with Eddie's daughter and they communicate all the time. Of the four of us, three are Italian and that's a really big connection. Having three Italians in the band created an incredibly familial, celebratory atmosphere that went on behind the scenes. When we weren't around, I picture the families getting together to break bread and saying, "What the hell is wrong with our kids?" They couldn't figure it out. Neither could I.

As I look back, the part of my life that still leaves me the saddest is the monumental mistake we, the Rascals, made in handling what really had become the part of our careers together—the publishing rights to our songs, those written by Eddie and me. It came during that time when Eddie wanted nothing to do with the band and was divesting himself of everything. The catalyst was when the late David Cassidy wanted to record our song "How Can I Be Sure?" His manager approached our people with an offer to buy the publishing rights to that song and everybody on our management side approved it. That started the ball rolling and it ended with us selling most of the publishing rights to all our songs. How that happened, I still don't know to this day, but I can only blame myself. When your advisors give you bad advice, you're dead—and we got bad advice. The prize in the music business, if you're fortunate, is the publishing part. Losing that still, honestly, upsets me. To this day, Eddie and I still haven't sat down and discussed that whole business, and I wish we could, if only for the sake of salvaging what little we have left of what we created together. But that's the "music business." If anyone ever tells you it's not about the money, they're not telling the truth. It's *only* about the money. It's sad but true. Take my word for it.

Chapter 9: The Hall of Fame

Despite all our internal troubles, there were those who pushed for us to be in the Rock and Roll Hall of Fame and that happened in 1997. Steve van Zandt of Bruce Springsteen's band was on the board, and he went out of his way to get the Rascals in there. Phil Spector was another one who was in our corner; he was adamant that we should be in there. There's no question that it's a big deal. Think of the people who never make it to that level. Being inducted should have been among the highlights of our careers. Instead, it just continued the level of vitriol that led to our break-up in the first place.

Here's how I remember that night. Steve van Zandt, who had worked so hard to get us into the Rock and Roll Hall of Fame in the first place, delivered an unbelievable introduction. It was funny. It was brilliant. It was respectful. He started out by saying, "Some people may not realize it, but the Rascals were the first rock and roll band in the world." He explained that okay, in the '50s there were vocal groups and in the '60s vocal groups and some solo artists, and, of course, on the west coast there were the Beach Boys, and in England some guys "were making some noise." But the first rock and roll band, said Steve, came from the "real world," from the "center of the universe, New Jersey." He added that he didn't understand why it took us so long to get into the Hall of Fame.

Steve recalled how he first saw us play at the Keyport Skating Rink in New Jersey, back when there were no stadiums, no Filmore's, when rock and roll was in skating rinks, "where it belonged." He mentioned our schoolboy outfits, the knickers and all that, and, at one point, took off his jacket to reveal he was wearing our signature look from the Young Rascals days.

He called Eddie a "wild man," jumping around on stage, and Gene was so "cool," he said, on guitar, while Dino was "the greatest rock drummer ever." He saved me for last, joking that "every roadie in New Jersey" hated me because they had hernias from having to pick up that "big thing," the Hammond B-3 and carry it on and off stage.

Everyone there that night heard from Steve van Zandt that when the Rascals were formed, New Jersey soul was born. "To sound that black, you had to be Italian," he told the audience, bringing the house down.

It was one hell of a moment.

For Steve himself, it was the start of a whole new career. That night producer David Chase saw his speech and was so impressed that he wanted to cast Steve in a new show for HBO titled "The Sopranos." That was especially cool because Steve had no acting experience. Imagine that. No acting experience, but he came across as so Italian that I guess they felt he'd really fit in. Before the actual induction itself, the organizers had asked us to perform. The whole thing wasn't just showing up at the event. We had a rehearsal period of about four or five days. Fortunately, Arif was still alive at the time and having him helped keep the temperature down between us. It was a good thing he was there.

Right away, the troubles began. I wanted this to be a joyous occasion. Part of that was I really wanted Chuck Rainey, one of the bass players on the Rascals records, to be a part of this performance. I was voted down. Finally, we used a bass player from another band. Again, stupidity started to happen on what should have been one of the most special nights of our lives.

After Steve van Zandt introduced us, the acceptance speeches started out okay. Dino went first and thanked our families and friends who, over the years, had shown us such great support. He called the award "such a wonderful honor."

Next came Gene, who thanked his mom, God, and Sid Bernstein, who, he said was right: that we had a pretty good band. He ended by thanking the fans and ending with "God bless you."

So far, so good.

Eddie looked at me, and I motioned to him to go next. The next thing I knew I thought my brain was going to blow up. I've been told that Eddie didn't want to stand next to me, even on the same side of the stage. I honestly don't remember, but I don't doubt it. What I do remember is that Eddie showed up looking like an American Indian, dressed in what appeared to be a buckskin jacket with fringe and turquoise jewelry around his collar.

He told the audience, "I'm talkin' here. Steve van Zandt said I could talk here." Then, he went on to thank our families and our friends before adding this: "We had a lot more magic and, uh, we had enough." Nobody was quite sure what Eddie was talking about, me included.

Here we were being honored in a place that most people consider to be the apex of musical achievement—the Rock and Roll Hall of Fame—and yet the nonsense continued. I was really proud to be there, but the behavior of my band-mates—and not only over the bass playing issue-really hurt.

Going last, I tried to salvage at least some of the night. First, I thanked Arif, who was in attendance, for all the help he gave the Rascals, Tom Dowd, and Ahmet Ertegun, Atlantic Records' president. Then I pointed out that "It was a great family in those days. And the fun that we had was shared by all of you because we were having it at the same time." It was all true and straight from the heart. Before I left the stage, I asked the audience's indulgence: "I've just got a little thing I'd like to say, if you don't mind.

What I said next is the very essence of what I believe, and I was proud, more than proud, privileged to have the forum in which to say it on that special night:

You know, one of the most important dates for the Rascals was July 20th, 1968, when "People Got to Be Free" became a number one hit in America. Number one, numero uno. But the truly important dates that year were ones that, in fact, inspired this song, April 4th, when Dr. King was killed, and when we lost Bobby Kennedy on

June 6. We wanted our music to be more than pop; wanted it to reach across races and social barriers, to help all of us understand each other a little better. That's what our music was all about. As timely as those sentiments were in '68, we believe they're even more vital right now. We seem to be still divided after all these years, rich from poor, and black from white. If we have one hope, and to accept this award, have one request, it's that all the artists who listen to this speech or program, who create tomorrow's music, tomorrow's hit songs, will use the music to reach out and heal, and bring us all closer together. Thank you very much.

I figured that was that. Night over. Eddie wasn't through, however.

After the ceremony, there was a press conference. Lots of media, lots of questions. Eddie used the platform to speak out against the music industry. He launched a complete verbal attack. All I remember was that he especially went after EMI, the music publishing company, and the music publishing industry in general. I tried to suggest to Eddie that he had to be careful, that there are libel laws in this country, and that he should tone it down. Instead, being Eddie, he went on to insult some of the major players in the music business by name, all of them multi-millionaires, some of them present in the room.

He was a real loose cannon that night, speaking without filter, with no safety valve. So, I had to sit by and watch him rant about how he was pissed off at the music business. Talk about a way to spoil a night. To this day, I still sometimes ask myself why that was necessary. Why did he have to turn such a wonderful night into a mixture of sugar and salt?

But I refuse to let my memories of that evening be ruined by what went wrong. I'd rather remember what went right. For one thing, it was the last time I saw Michael Jackson and all of the Bee Gees together. I'm glad I went for that and other reasons. God put me with these guys and in this place, and I was damn well not going to let anything get in the way of the joy. I was happy to have my family, including my sister Fran, and my daughters, Aria, Christina, and Laura, there with me. We had fun, even though I think I passed out from exhaustion. There's so much about our induction that still sticks with me. Let's start with the improbability of it all. For four kids to go from where we were and get where we did is pretty miraculous. Not too many reach such a pinnacle. My friend Eddie Money—who left us last year, leaving behind a terrific catalog in his own right, may he forever rest peacefully—used to joke with me all the time. He'd call me at least once a year and say, "Come on, Felix, help me get in the Hall so my kids won't think I'm a bum."

I wish I could've helped, but that's not how it works. Truth is, there are a lot of deserving people who don't make it to the Rock and Roll Hall of Fame. It's a long list. It's not always about talent, but, especially these days, it has more to do with the fact that it has become a television event. They want inductees who will draw the biggest audience. At least that's my opinion.

Because the Rock and Roll Hall of Fame gets so much attention every year and they have this massive building in Cleveland, it really stands out in most people's minds when they think of the Rascals, collectively or individually. It's in all the advertising for shows, as in "Rock and Roll Hall of Fame member Felix Cavaliere," and comes up in nearly every interview I do.

What so many people either forget or aren't aware of is that there are other wonderfully significant ways in which Eddie and I and the Rascals have been honored.

One is the Songwriters Hall of Fame. Most fans don't know a lot about this Hall of Fame partly because its inductions aren't televised, but it's a huge deal to me that I'm in it. It was started by the great songwriter Johnny Mercer, and there are so many greats are in there. Gamble and Huff, who I so respect, are the co-chairmen.

Kenny Gamble and Leon Huff are two of the finest musicians and human beings I've ever had the privilege of meeting. They are true gentlemen as well as being giants in our business. Gamble and Huff started out around the same time as the Rascals and had a profound influence on me, my songwriting, and my music—and I wasn't alone. These two geniuses wrote and produced some of the best songs ever: "The Love I Lost" by Harold Melvin and the Blue Notes, "Backstabbers" and "Love Train" by the Ojays, "Me and Mrs. Jones" by Billy Paul—the list goes on and on. Records by the Three Degrees ("When Will I See You Again?") to Lou Rawls and Jerry Butler. All together, they were responsible for 15 gold singles and 22 gold albums. That's a lot of talent that might not have ever gotten there without Gamble and Huff.

I've always felt that Gamble and Huff and the Rascals shared a lot in common besides music. Our philosophies were very similar. In an interview for the Rock and Roll Hall of Fame (they were inducted in 2008), Kenny Gamble is quoted as saying "We wanted to take social themes and translate them to commercial recordings. Philadelphia International was about spreading love." He also said, in another interview, "That's what our whole thing was, what all our music was about: people uniting, living together in peace and harmony and having fun." That sounds an awful lot like what I wanted to do with the Rascals and what I still try to do in my solo career.

The Songwriters Hall of Fame is, or was, at that time, a very select group of people. In order to be considered for induction, you had to get a "push" from others in the industry. They have to put you on the "A-list." I got a call one day from Karen Sherry, an executive at ASACP (the music publishing trade group) and she said "Felix, are you sitting down? How would you like to be inducted into the Songwriters Hall of Fame?" Are you Joking?! I had tears in my eyes. This is a very special honor. The people inducted into this organization are the finest in the history of popular music.

Naturally, Eddie also received a call informing him of the invitation to be inducted. I'm told that he said he wouldn't go unless his brother, David, could also be there.

So, the night came in 2009 when Eddie and I were inducted. Not only did Eddie want his brother, David, present, he also wanted him on stage with us. Remember, during all our years together, Eddie never told me, Gene, or Dino that David had helped Eddie with the lyrics to some of the songs. All we knew was that he had sung background vocals on some of our records. It was another strange night. Here we were—Eddie and I—on stage and there was his brother, David, who wasn't a recipient, but who also gave a speech. It was awkward, to say the least, however, despite all that, it was another extremely special night in my life.

I remain extremely proud of the songs we wrote together—more so as I continue to hear other amazing versions. Obviously, not only the Rascals' versions of those songs have stood the test of time, but many have been recorded by other artists over the years, including some incredible "standouts." To me, the definition of a good song is one that can be translated into several different genres, and variety of styles. What really constitutes a great song for me is that you can do it as a cocktail song, jazz, salsa, or rap. It's great to hear how others do our songs. First of all, it makes you feel validated because someone else liked your song enough to want to play and sing it, even though so much time has passed since you wrote it.

None of the versions I'll mention are imitations of what we did but are really good and different interpretations. Going way back, Aretha recorded "Groovin" a couple of years after our original rendition. Olivia Newtown-John did a really good version of "How Can I Be Sure?" a few years ago. A French singer named Nicoletta did a version of the same song that sold two million copies in France and another version in Canada, also entirely in French, went to number one there.

One of my favorite versions of our songs was the Fifth Dimension's version of "People Got to Be Free" in 1970. They did something really interesting with the arrangement, putting it together in a medley with Sam Cooke's song "A Change is Gonna Come." A more recent version of "People Got to Be Free" was done by Mark Stein, lead singer and keyboardist of the group Vanilla Fudge.

Mark has been kind enough to say that what he calls my "massive sound" on the Hammond B-3 influenced him to get into music; he even tells people he studied my playing at different clubs back in the '60s, which is really a compliment. The list of those who have done our songs goes on and on, but I guess that's more than enough for anyone's bucket list!

So, just for a moment, imagine what it means to a songwriter to be invited into the same rarified company as the great songwriters of all-time, people ranging from Cole Porter to George Gershwin. I have a story about my "close call" with Gershwin—okay, not exactly with him, since he passed many years ago, but a connection to him. It happened a few years after my induction into the Songwriters Hall of Fame.

I was invited to testify in Washington in support of songwriters' royalties, something that is increasingly important in this digital age of streaming music. It was a memorable event on several fronts. First, it was one of the last times both sides—Republicans and Democrats—were able to get together in the same place and listen to each other on the same issue.

But it was also when I got to play the great George Gershwin's piano. There are actually two pianos. One is in the ASCAP building in New York City and the other at the Library of Congress in Washington. Well, after my testimony that day in Washington, there was a nice luncheon, and I was asked if I would like to see George Gershwin's piano. Is that possible? How many ways could I say "yes, please?"

The piano itself is all roped off, obviously protected due to its historical value. They removed the ropes, and I was able to play a little on the keyboard. For all I know, these are the same keys on which Gershwin composed "Rhapsody in Blue" or "American in Paris." Very few people, except for Gershwin himself ever had their fingers on that piano's keyboard. Stevie Wonder, I believe, is another. What rarified company!Induction into the Grammy Hall of Fame was another great honor. "Groovin" was selected for inclusion in 1999, which makes me extremely proud, given that Atlantic never wanted to release it in the first place. Thank God for Murray the K sticking up for that record. In 2005, the Rascals were inducted into the Vocal Group Hall of Fame. The list of luminaries in that group is unbelievable, including the Beatles, the Supremes, the Four Tops, and going way back, many of the vocal groups I grew up listening to and wanting to be like.

The Hammond Hall of Fame is limited to those who play my instrument, the Hammond organ, and includes others like the late Billy

Preston (with whom I played many, many times), Steve Winwood, Al Kooper, Booker T. Jones, and, going way back, Fats Waller.

And finally, the Musician's Hall of Fame founded here in Nashville by Joe Chambers, a true gentleman whose enthusiasm for music and devotion towards its players is nothing short of inspiring.

All of these honors mean a lot to me, mainly because I know how much they would mean to my mother. God rest her soul. And I always think of how much seeing her son celebrated in this way would have meant to her. Like I said, that kid taking piano lessons still lives inside me.

Chapter 10: On Stage Once More

Over the years, we tried—and many others, on our behalf have tried—to put together a Rascals reunion. There were always reasons why it couldn't and didn't happen. Most of them had to do with Eddie and some of them no doubt had to do with money.

First, Eddie really didn't want to tour; he didn't want to go out on the road. I'm probably not the only person, and maybe not the best person to answer the question of why. However, one of my friends from the old Pelham neighborhood, Tommy Calagna, who I've known since I was about five, put it this way: "Ego and fear." What he meant was Eddie didn't want to admit he couldn't perform anymore, and he really has a deathly fear of airplanes. He also really didn't like being away from his family.

I think Tommy knows what he's talking about. He's known me longer than I've known any of the Rascals. His brother, John, who sadly passed away at the young age of 34, was the kid in line ahead of me in school who asked "Hey, you like rock and roll?" Tommy has been there with me all through the Rascals days and right up to the present. I respect his opinion because he's a true friend.

In the over 40 years since the Rascals broke up, throughout all those years, Eddie hasn't done much in music. He made one album—one album—in all those years. Okay, so I agree with this idea: if you don't want to be in the music business, don't be in the music business. If you don't want to do it, don't do it. I have no problem with that.

There is a "comeback" of sorts that Eddie made in recent years, doing a show in New York and New Jersey called "Eddie Brigati: My Life After the Rascals," in which he does one of our songs, in addition to some show tunes. Again, though, it's in his backyard of New York and New Jersey and doesn't involve any touring.

There was one event—really a philanthropic cause—that would briefly bring Eddie, me, and the other Rascals back together after that night at the Rock and Roll Hall of Fame induction. Here's how it finally happened, from my perspective. I got a phone call one day from my daughter, Lisa. At that time, she and her husband owned a limo company that drove Bruce Springsteen, U-2, Paul McCartney, Neil Young, and others to and from their shows.

Lisa said, "Dad, don't get nervous. I've got a lump in my breast."

"Oh, no. Is it cancerous?"

"No, I don't think so." She was that kind of kid, always trying to be optimistic.

Not long after that, the phone rings again and it's Steve Van Zandt and he says, "You know every year, Bruce and I do this Kristin Carr benefit for cancer. It's $5,000 a ticket and we'll raise a lot of money. Why don't you get the Rascals back together and play the show?" I told him about Lisa. Steve knew her personally because, as I said, Springsteen used her company as drivers to his shows. He still does. So, Steve said, "Look, regardless of what happens we can certainly turn you on to the right physicians and the right treatments."

I thought to myself, you know, God's talking to me. Forget about all the other stuff, the blah, blah, blah. Whatever happened before with the Rascals… and with that, I told Steve to count me in.

We were only talking about one night, but that's how this all started as far as I'm concerned. So, we went into New York, all of us, we had a rehearsal with Paul Schaffer of David Letterman's band helping out, and the show was at the Tribeca Grill in New York City, Robert Di Nero's place. It was very well attended, just as Steve had predicted. People were happy to see the Rascals together again. The place was packed. And at five grand a ticket it raised a ton of money.

In addition to the four of us, Eddie had his brother, David, on stage and his wife, Susan, also took part as a singer. It was a small stage and we had Paul Shaffer up there as well and I thought that, musically, it was challenging. I was up on a riser in the back and couldn't really hear myself properly, not to mention that there were so many people on the stage, complicating matters.

But everybody loved it. They loved it. It just made me realize, in that moment, on that night, just how much music—our music—meant to people's lives. Given that it was later determined that my daughter Lisa did, in fact, have cancer, that night now has even more special meaning to me. I'm so glad we did it. I'm pleased to this day that we could put aside our differences and come together to help others in the way we did.

So, we did the show and I thought that was it. One night and it's over. But that wasn't the ending. I should have known better. It was really the beginning of this thing that would turn into a full-blown Broadway show and a one-year tour of the original Rascals. I'm not entirely sure how the discussions about doing the Broadway show began, except to say that I think Gene and Dino, who didn't share in the royalties from the Rascals' records, might have really been looking for a way to make a living. Either they hit on van Zandt to do it, or van Zandt hit on them. I'm not sure which it was, but here we were talking again about getting back together to play our music.

At that time, and since, I was making a nice living and I had, and still have the nicest band in the world. They're all fabulous Nashville musicians who have played and still play with some of the best artists on the planet, besides working with me as part of "Felix Cavaliere's Rascals." I'm so thrilled that I can say we've been together, at this point, for almost 20 years and we have never really had a problem in all that time. "I'm having a pretty damned good time," I said to the others, "so you've got to give me a real good reason why we should get back together beyond that one night." So, the conversations began, but I wasn't privy to all of them.

Let me say, first and foremost, that I want to enjoy my life, so it took a lot of convincing to get me to participate. Steve and his wife, Maureen van Zandt, were very persuasive. "You don't understand," they told me.

"We're going to do this; we're going to do that. We're going to be on Broadway." They really wanted this to happen. Steve made me a very substantial offer. We drew up a contract and I reluctantly signed it. Part of the reason was because my wife, Donna, really wanted to see it happen.

I have to say that in the beginning it sounded like a pretty good idea, but maybe too ambitious and too expensive to be sustainable. Before the show ever got to Broadway, we played some performances at the Capitol Theater in Port Chester, New Jersey. They were sold out and the excitement built some momentum for our Broadway run, which was really only for a few weeks. Then, we hit the road on a national tour in May of 2013.

The show's whole concept, as Steve van Zandt once described it, was like "Jersey Boys," with the exception that, in his vision, the actual Four Seasons would have been in it, playing and singing all the songs. There were actors, prerecorded, appearing on big video screens behind us, portraying us as kids and telling the story of how we'd become a band. We also had a backing group of a keyboard player, a bass player, and three backup singers. Still, the Rascals sound was front and center and that was the important thing—both to the fans and to us. At least that's how I saw it, maybe because that's how I wanted it to be. Maybe it's because that's how I've always wanted it to be!

The Broadway run was great, but the cracks started to show once we got on the road. Some cities on the multi-night tour were sold out, but most had a good number of empty seats. Three nights in Boston could be full, but in Phoenix you could see the empty chairs. It's hard to fill seats three nights in a row in the same city. It was an incredibly fabulous show that was just not economically feasible. Eventually, the tour fell under its own weight. Without notice, the show's producers decided to pull the plug.

Everybody in the show, including us, found out by e-mail that it was over.

Let it be known that none of us had anything to do with the cancellation of the tour. We were just told that it was over. Okay, so that's the bad part. There was a lot of good stuff about getting back together, though. For one thing, for the most part, once the group started playing together, we all got along. We were helped a lot, no doubt, by the fact that we all had our wives there.

That really helped as most of us prefer to not act like a jerks around our wives. We really tried to "make nice" and, for the most part, we succeeded.

I hesitate to go into all the negatives about it because we had a great time. Look at it this way: we did Broadway; in fact, we packed Broadway for almost two weeks. I was in a theater, the Richard Rodgers Theater, where they had done the original "South Pacific" and "Oklahoma." I considered that an honor. We had people who were flying in from Europe and Asia to attend the show.

It was really nice to feel the love and see the way people embraced the idea that the Rascals were back together. The show was well done with this genius, Mark Brickman, who did the videos. He also had an extremely modern type of presentation. A lot of the theaters today have been retrofitted with cameras all over the ceilings, leading to images on giant screens. So, that part was great. The technology was fabulous.

I also got the chance to see how groups go out on the road today, compared to in our day. When the Broadway run ended and we took the show across America, we had 22 people with us. It's a whole different ballgame from what we were used to in the past. This is how big groups go out and tour today. It's not just them, but a whole team of people responsible for every little thing you see and hear. They go out like an army. There was a lot of new technology that I had never used before, such as high-quality ear monitors (kind of like a hearing aid in each ear that allows you to hear yourself and the other musicians as you're all playing). There was this huge, bigger-than-life screen behind us. It was an interesting experience to relive our music in such fashion.

As I say, as far as the actual band, goes, we really didn't have a problem. We never had an argument. We never had a disagreement. There was just a really interesting relationship between those of us on stage and the hierarchy on the production side. I mentioned Mark Brickman, a person who I really do think is a "genius" at what he does, but he was put in charge as a partner in the whole enterprise and that was a flaw. He knows everything about lighting; he even did the lights on the Empire

State Building. But that doesn't mean he knew how to do the nuts and bolts of a production—by that I mean what to do in terms of people getting along with one another.

None of this is to suggest I didn't like being a part of it. There were many nights when I did. One thing that really stood in the way of my enjoyment, though, was the need for everything to be so regimented. Songs had to be played exactly the same way every night, with no deviation. That was a necessity because they had to synch up with the video effects that were preprogrammed to come on at a precise time. For a creative person, that's really like being put in a box. For me, it was frustrating because I like to improvise and experiment and that just couldn't happen. My own opinion is that what people really wanted to see was just us, the four original Rascals playing on stage. That's just my opinion, but a lot of critics of the show seem to have agreed.

Most were kind and complimentary, but others saw the show as a concert masquerading as a play.

One reviewer for Billboard called it "a good concert, but a poor theatrical production." The reviewer went on to add: "It's nice that the Rascals are together after 40 years. Bands do that all the time. They just don't try to turn it into a Broadway show." Many other critics said similar things, which is a shame considering how much time, effort, and money went into producing the show. One review, however, hit the nail on the head, stating that the play wasn't the thing, the music was. And he said the music was very, very good.

The story line of the play really kind of glossed over a lot of the big issues that caused us to break up and that's unfortunate. There's nothing about drugs or competition or ego. There was a lot of the "real" story missing. Given that, we would have been better off sticking to the music, which was what pretty much all the show's reviews said in common.

So, it was about the music, right? That's what everybody said, but the van Zandt version of our life story—something he called a "bio-concert"—didn't emphasize that music as much as I think, in retrospect, that it should have; that's ultimately what, I believe, brought it down, but there's no question there were great moments during the show.

Eddie, for example, got a standing ovation almost every night on "How Can I Be Sure?" The first night on Broadway the sound went a little bad through the first two songs and he was hard to hear, but from there on out, especially when we hit the road, he was killing that song every night. Gene probably never played guitar better; he's really a better guitar player now, as I've told him directly, than he was back in our time with the Rascals.

Every one of us still had it. By that, I mean, let's face it: we're older. But all the reviews, even the ones that weren't the most complimentary, said that we still had it, musically. And we did. We really did. Another example is Dino. When he first started playing in rehearsals for the show, he really wasn't very good. But then he changed his style. He had changed his feel in those years since the Rascals disbanded. He really wasn't playing with other people. He was playing by himself. You have to climb up the hill and keep improving, playing with people who are at least as good, hopefully even better, than you are. Time away from that process doesn't help.

As fans, I think we all realize what great drumming brings to rock and roll music. So, that happened as the tour went on. Dino really started to key into the playing. Another thing that happened was an article came out in *Drummer* magazine while we were on tour. Suddenly, Dino realized that all the people who were successful in the drumming business wrote into the magazine talking about how they owed so much of their success to him—that he had been their inspiration. He must have realized something along the lines of "Hey, I'm fricking Dino Danelli and I'm going to start playing like it." And he took off! His drumming soared. I'll tell you something: when Dino Danelli plays drums like only Dino Danelli can, he's hard to beat. He's a great showman with great ability; it was an absolute joy to see him play drums again.

To me, the biggest disappointment was that we were never really free to play like I know we could and, I believe, still can. We all sounded good, especially for a group of musicians who hadn't worked together in over 40 years. But the "vehicle," the play, just didn't connect with the music. People didn't come out, spend their hard-earned money (tickets were up to $150 in some places we played) to see a so-called "bio-concert." They wanted to see the Rascals— the band they remembered from their youth. Here we were, right there on stage, the original guys, and they just wanted us to play, without all the interruptions. On the other hand, let's keep in mind that Steve and Maureen didn't start out wanting it not to work. Their intentions, I'm certain, were good.

You have to remember that Steve van Zandt talked about going to his first Rascals concert as a teenager and falling in love. He was personally invested, in more than just money.

I believe he wanted it to work. His heart was in the right place and I think it was on his bucket list to see the Rascals together again. Like so many in the audience at those shows, it took him back to his youth.

So, the fans connected with the music and that was the wonderful part. Like the song that started the show every night, "It's Wonderful," some nights it really was.

But my wife, who's very wise, has pointed out that it's difficult to get back together after so many years; it was a little like being with your "ex" again. All four of us are really creative guys and it's hard to be put in the same box every night and not be allowed to improvise and stretch your creative talents. Everything was fine before and after the show, but sometimes, in the middle, all the same old emotions would come back, the same stuff that broke us up in the first place.

I thank Steve Van Zandt for what he did to reunite us. He gave us a tremendous amount of publicity, exposed our music to the whole world and I had, for the most part, a good time when we were playing. And there were several great surprises along the way. One of the biggest was the day Steve called me and said, "I got something to show you, Felix. Come into my studio; you got to come into the studio." So, I followed him, going into the studio where he played this little piece of video tape where Eddie thanks me for writing all the songs and takes the blame for breaking up the group.

If you saw "Once Upon a Dream," you'll remember that moment. I looked at Steve and said, "So, how the hell did you pull this one off?" When that piece of tape of Eddie apologizing made it into the show, I got a standing ovation. I'm not sure if it was sincere or just show business on Eddie's part, but the crowd loved it.

There's business and there's show business. Suffice to say, one thing I have learned over the years is that there are good businessmen and good musicians. Not too many people can be both. It's a problem for all musicians, all creative people. Your heart is one thing; your head is another. It's a left-right brain thing.

You can't take a band that, at that time, was 47 years old, unless it's a mega-band, like say Led Zeppelin, and try to fill a place with a $150,000 - $175,000 show five nights a week. It isn't going to happen. It might happen in New York, but it's not going to happen in Phoenix.

Things just started to break down. You have to have a bottom line in terms of earnings. It was like a big passion project, one that lost millions, a lot of money by anybody's standards.

The tour ended on my 72nd birthday. Two days, later, I called and said to each of them—Dino, Gene, and Eddie's wife, Susan—look we have a little momentum going here. "Once Upon a Dream" ended, I told them, but we can still go out and do our show, the Rascals show. We can do it ourselves and make money. I took a meeting with Steve Martin, the president of the talent agency APA, who wanted to put it together. He had seen "Once Upon a Dream" and told me, in his opinion, it could have been run differently. He confirmed that the demand to see us play together as a group, not as part of a "play," was still out there. Gratified by that, I waited and waited to hear back from Eddie.

That call never came. When I first called, his wife said he was at the post office and he'd call me back. Two years later, he never called me back. I now joke about how, once again, I screwed things up with Eddie. I used the wrong word. I said, "Do you want to come out and work?"

What I should have said was, "Do you want to come out and play?"

Gene and Dino kind of said yes, but Dino wanted to go out on the road with the same show that had just closed down because it lost tons of money. I said to him, "Dino, let me ask you something. Do you want to make money, or do you want to lose money? I'm not being facetious. We know how to lose money. Just put that show on."

I explained that first of all, we don't own that show. Second, people don't want that show. They want the Rascals. They want the original Rascals, playing together, the way we know how to play, without all the special effects, video, and everything else that gets in the way of the music. Then, there's the other line I love. I was told by the others, "We don't want to go out as an oldies band." My response was, "Hey, have you seen a calendar recently? That was 1965. What do you think we are? Kids?" I get a kick out of that: "We don't want to go out as an oldies band." Here it was rearing its ugly head again: Ego.

Speaking of ego, it's not confined to musicians and entertainers. My current manager, Obi Steinman, went through hell trying to get us back together. Many managers have what I call the businessman's ego, which says, "I can do this. Nobody else can do this. I can do this." I said to him, "You really think so? Okay, if you think you have to do this, go ahead." After months and months of trying, Obi came back and said, "You know Felix, I'll never doubt you again."

To be honest, at one point, I said to Steve Martin, whose agency really wanted to put the tour together, "how about if I get the other two, would that work?" It's obvious that Eddie doesn't want to come out, so how about three Rascals? I still couldn't even get the three of us together. So, we have a band, and, as my manager says to this day, don't use the "R" word with me anymore. It's like the "N" word to him now. Just don't use it, he tells me or he'll quit. He's kidding. I think.

My response is always along the lines of "now you know. I told you you've never met guys like this." If we had played it right, out of what was proposed as a four-million-dollar tour we might have made, say several hundred thousand each, after expenses—decent money for a trio in their seventies. You're so blessed when FIFTY years later, people still want to hear your music.

For one thing, think about this. How many other rock groups exist from our era, of our generation, where *all* the original members are still alive? Not many. The Beatles? No. The Rolling Stones? No. The Who? No. The Beach Boys? Not by a longshot. Keep going. Seriously, we're pretty much it. So here we are, the last rock and roll group from the sixties and seventies where all the original members are still walking this earth and can still play the songs they made famous and can still sound good doing it. Why wouldn't people want to come out and see that? The bigger question is, why can't we get it together and give the people what they want? Why can't we bring that joy and be grateful that we still can? It just doesn't make sense to me.

I always had this conceptual idea of a singing group that could really play. You have to understand that was the driving force behind the Rascals. That's what I really wanted to do. When it happened, it really was a dream come true; that's one reason I named that album "Once Upon a Dream." Because it happened. Here were these four kids, all from the east coast of America, who decided to take on the British Invasion. And then we did it. We survived, we delivered, and then we self-destructed. To me, it's like a minor Greek tragedy. It's a shame that we lost it. When are we going to get an opportunity to be around a situation where we could give so much joy ever again?

Things are even more complicated because the families behind us were all good people. Most of them have passed away, but they were all hard-working sons-of-a-gun. All of a sudden, their kids came into some money and started putting them all up, buying them houses. Well, had we stayed together, we'd have had something not just to give our parents and our kids, but all of our grandkids, too. It wouldn't be just for us, but all the people we love and who love us. There's never been a time when I haven't had my kids' backs. I always say: if you don't believe God's got your back, know that I've got your back. You're not going to fall down the hill; don't worry. I've got your back. There was a time when I felt that way about the Rascals: that we had each other's backs. I wish it had been true.

I've always felt that someone was watching out for me on this earth. Either you grow up like that or you don't. If you don't, then you probably grow up believing the world is going to crash into you. The others might not have grown up the way I did, believing that others have your back. I'm sure it's hard for them to see things from my perspective. They didn't all come from the background in which I was raised, and which allows me to see things in a different way. I feel fortunate for my upbringing and I'm not going to apologize for that. I sometimes think the others resented me for that—having the chance to go to college, for one thing. Somebody up there liked me and I'm grateful.

When I close my eyes and sing, to this day, I still can see us together back then. When a group is successful, it's magical. Gene uses that word. I use that word. It's hard to know what I mean if you haven't felt that kind of magic. It's like being on an all-star team. It doesn't mean you're going to win the championship every year, but it does mean you're around a group that, when we play, it's happening. And that's how it was on the "Once Upon a Dream" tour when we played together again after forty years; that's the part that really made it fun. Some of our fellow musicians felt it, too. Paul Shaffer, who I greatly respect, saw the show in New York before we hit the road and he loved it. He thought we were even better than back in 1964. He thought we sounded "magnificent" and that Gene, especially, has gotten even better over the years.

I was proud that, as we got toward the third or fourth month out on the road, things really gelled. And whatever it is people loved about the Rascals came out on stage. All that love, all that joy, just came back and we felt it every night in every city. If you went to any of the shows, you know what I'm talking about. The word magic just keeps coming up, because it was all of that— magic of the kind you sometimes, if you're lucky to be a part of it, only experience once in a lifetime or, as the title goes, "Once Upon a Dream."

Personally and professionally, it took me a long time to get back to work with my current band—"Felix Cavaliere's Rascals"—after the "Once Upon a Dream" tour ended. I had lost a lot of solo bookings because I'd agreed not to play for eight months as a term of being a part of the reunion tour. That's a long time in this business. I will say that it was a nice break and a serious upgrade to play quality shows with ideal lighting and sound as well as nice accommodations and transportation. But I also was happy to get back to being me, Felix Cavaliere. Once the dust settled, I felt very hopeful because I sensed there was so much ahead, so much to which I could look forward. To put it bluntly, I felt free again.

I hope I can continue to bring back memories for people and, at the same time, build new ones for myself and my family—my children and grandchildren, especially. It may be that the Rascals will never be together again, and if that's how it is, then that's okay. I'm fine with it. But I'll go on, in part because I always have, somewhat because I have to, and, most importantly, because I want to do what I do for as long as I can.

Music is not only what I do. It is who I am.

Chapter 11: Today and Tomorrow

As I reflect on my life, beginning with the early days in Pelham, the Catskills, playing with Joey Dee in Europe, and ultimately forming the Rascals, I can't help but think about how much I've seen and how much has changed. Music, the music industry, the world… Think about it. Just in terms of technology, we've gone from tape to vinyl, from vinyl to CD, from CD to DVD, and from all of the above to streaming. Not to mention that now we're coming back around to vinyl! And who knows what's next? Whatever it is, I'm sure it will be interesting, because everything evolves.

Not only have I had a front-row seat witnessing it all, but I'm blessed to still be here now. You see, I've never stopped making music over the last half-century. If you really think about it, the time I spent as a Rascal really adds up to a very small part of my 50-year career as a musician and songwriter. It amounts to roughly the years between 1965 and 1972. Those latter years didn't even include all four of us, so the original Rascals really ended much earlier. The songs, however, have lived on, and as the audience grows older, you just really hope they keep playing the music of our generation at home, so their kids and grandkids grow up on it. It's really gratifying to see several generations in my audiences on some nights—parents, their children or even grandchildren.

Radio helps keep our music out there, especially the classic stations that play music of the '60s and '70s. Remember so-called "Oldies" stations? They still exist, thank God, but there are fewer and fewer of them and as another decade passes, another gets labeled as classic. Still, people hear our songs everyday all over the world, whether on radio, streaming, person collections, in movie soundtracks, or on commercials. "It's a Beautiful Morning" was in a McDonald's TV commercial in 1988 and one for Days Inn in the early '90s. I have no idea just how many film soundtracks "Groovin" has been in, but I know it's a lot and I'm also told that, most recently, it was the title track on a jazz album and on the soundtrack of a film called "I'll See You in My Dreams" in 2015. And maybe you've heard it on the Subway commercials for their Rueben sandwich (with "Rueben" sung to the melody of "Groovin").

So, that's mainly how I'm known, for those songs and as a Rascal and that's fine with me. I never really intended to be a solo artist or a singer, for that matter. I was always happy being in the background on stage coordinating the music.

I remember vividly one of my first shows without the Rascals. It was in the Catskills, a place called the Browns Hotel. People in the audience were looking for the other Rascals, especially Eddie. In fact, it wasn't uncommon, some nights, for someone in the audience to yell out, "Where's Eddie?" I'd just smile and yell back, "he's home!" What else could I say? He was gone, and here I was on my own.

It took me awhile to go from the back of the band to the front. It was an evolution. There's just no handbook to teach you how to perform. Think about it. You can take lessons to learn how to be a better musician, but who teaches anybody how to be a better performer?

Nobody. I think of it this way. In baseball, how do you learn how to hit a fastball? You practice, that's how. You can't just go up there and hit a home run the first time. You have to miss the ball quite a few times and then practice until you get better at it. It's that simple, but it's harder than it sounds. It's work. If you keep at it, you can improve and get better. It's always gratifying when I hear critics say my voice today is as good as when I was 25. None of us are who we were when we were 25, but I try to pace myself, both on and off stage.

Thankfully, I've had a very productive solo career, amounting to more albums than I recorded with the Rascals. The first was in 1974, simply called "Felix Cavaliere." It was produced by Todd Rundgren on the Bearsville label, founded in 1970 by Albert Grossman, who at various times managed giants like Bob Dylan, Janis Joplin, the Band, and Peter, Paul, and Mary. He decided one day to start his own record label and I was part of it. A number of great musicians were on that album, including wonderful jazz trumpet player Randy Brecker and the brilliant voice of Cissy Houston, Whitney's mother. I co-wrote the songs with Carman Moore, who like me, is a classically trained musician. We used just about every instrument you can imagine on that album: clarinet, flamenco guitar, pedal steel guitar, baritone horns, cello, viola, violins, and congas. It was like the old days working at Atlantic with Arif; it became a musical stretch by allowing me to try out new things while using approaches that had worked well in the past.

I produced and recorded an album entitled "Castles in the Air" in 1979. With the marvelously talented Luther Vandross backing me on some of the vocals. The album also included a beautiful, stripped-down version of "People Got to Be Free." I'm proud of that album. It also was released in Japan on the Epic label, where it found great success producing a hit single called "Only a Lonely Heart Sees," which made it to #2 on Billboard magazine's Adult Contemporary charts in 1980. I still think it's one of my most underrated songs. It's just a wonderful piece of music and lyrics that I wish more people heard it back then and listened to it today.

I recorded "Dreams in Motion" (1994), produced by the great Don Was, and recorded two albums with Steve Cropper, a founding member of Booker T. and the MG's: "Nudge It Up a Notch" (2008), a Grammy nominated album of which I'm both proud of and humbled by, and "Midnight Flyer" (2010), released on the Stax record label, known for recording groups like old friends Sam and Dave, Booker T. and the MG's, Isaac Hayes. Steve still plays as part of the "Blues Brothers" act on the road. He's also in the Rock and Roll Hall of Fame, inducted in 1992, along with the MG's. It was a great pleasure to work with Steve, the man who wrote songs like "Knock on Wood," "In the Midnight Hour" (which I recorded back on the first Rascals' album and still perform today), and "Dock of the Bay" for Otis Redding.

Steve and I both live in Nashville, so collaborating was as easy as it was wonderful. We recorded it in Jon Tivens' home studio and the three of us co-wrote most of the songs on "Nudge It Up a Notch." We had the great drummer Chester Thompson, who has played with Geneses as well as Frank Zappa. Not to mention being the drummer of "Weather Report," one of the great jazz bands of our time. The former Impressions bassist Sammy Louis "Shake" Anderson was also part of those sessions. "Nudge" was nominated for a Grammy as well as receiving some great reviews.

The second album we did together, "Midnight Flyer." The highlight for me was recording the song "I Can Stand It." Where I performed a duet with my daughter Aria.

While I was doing all this writing and recording, I was also producing the music of other artists. I've mentioned Laura Nyro before. Again, the purest artist I've ever met, heard, or seen. She knew exactly what she wanted from every song she wrote. She had a vision for all of her songs and wanted them to be just the way she heard them within. The musicians we hired from Muscle Shoals and New York respected her every wish. They played every nuance she wanted. Adding to the experience was Duane Allman contributing his magical guitar. It was a wonderful experience for all of us.

I was privileged to produce several of her albums, the first "Christmas and the Beads of Sweat" in 1970. We were accompanied by the Muscle Shoals Group and Duane Allman on guitar. Another great thrill! The album was co-produced, as I mentioned, with Arif Mardin, which certainly added to the great joy of working with such brilliant musicians.

Laura and I had come a long way since she and I first met when introduced by her then-manager, David Geffen. We came to trust each other's musical judgment and that made our collaborations so much more special. Laura lent her vocal talents to one of the tracks on my "Destiny" album, "Love Came." She was magical and majestic in her writing and her music. The fact that I got to produce her album is among the highlights of my post-Rascals' life and career. Just knowing her as a person was such a big part of both my music and my life.

In 1986 I had the privilege of playing with Willie Nelson at one of the first Farm Aid concerts. So many great names appeared on that amazing venue holding such precious meaning for the great, great people of our country's heartland. I did the Curtis Mayfield song "People Get Ready" in addition to "People Got to Be Free." That year the concert was held in Austin and there are two things that I remember about the experience. One was that it was hot as hell and the other is that it was the last time I saw Stevie Ray Vaughn play. I was playing solo, just me and a piano and I had to follow Stevie Ray and his band "Double Trouble." Not easy on any day, let alone following the set they laid down that afternoon, their energy, their commitment to a crowd that was in need of hosing down—It was so hot—Stevie Ray and his band gave it everything. It was inspiring. Stevie Ray died four years later, after the plane in which he was a passenger crashed on takeoff. He was only 35 and had so much more to give musically.

On a brighter note, thinking about Willie reminds me of what a truly fine gentleman he is, someone who really cares and really gives of himself to others. I met him for the first time when I lived back in Danbury, Connecticut, where his manager, Mark Rothbaum also lived, and have always thought highly of him as a person and as a talent.

Another part of my solo journey since the days of the Rascals has involved working alongside other legendary people like Ringo Starr, of whom I spoke earlier, but his "largesse" bears repeating. In 1992, I was a member of that aptly named "All-Starr Band," What a time. Playing alongside a Beatle was an honor, as was playing alongside John Entwistle of the Who, Randy Bachman of Bachman-Turner Overdrive, Mark Farner from Grand Funk, Mark Rivera, the great sax player from Billy Joel's band, and Billy Preston who many have tabbed the "fifth Beatle."

Playing the "All-Starr" tour finally landed me in Japan, something I'd always wanted to do with the Rascals, but for reasons I've talked about earlier, it never happened. The Japanese people are such great fans. They love the music and, you know what? While some don't even know English, they know the lyrics to all the songs. That was evident when I first played there with my "Felix Cavaliere's Rascals" group in 2010. I had it proven to me again in 2016, when I played for a week in Tokyo with my current band. We did two clubs there, "the Cotton Club" and "the

Blue Note." I can never stress enough how great the Japanese audiences are to artists.

Picture this: you're all the way around the world and they know the words to the songs, they've been listening to your music since they were like 15 or 16 years old. After the shows, they come up for an autograph and in their arms, they hold stacks of like 10 brand new CDs for me to sign. I'd never even seen some of these albums. They were all reprints made specifically for the Asian market. The Japanese are extremely attuned to our music and really appreciate some of the songs that were never even hits in the U.S. In fact, the "Peaceful World" album we did for Columbia was, and still is, a favorite in Japan. In 1970, when it first came out, there were no CD's, of course. However, "Peaceful World" was voted by the Japanese public the album they most wanted to be reproduced on CD. I'm very proud of that.

The Japanese audiences were great, but so were the people for whom we were working. The treatment was just wonderful. I've got to compose some sort of a letter one of these days for our fan base and for all the people over there that are so supportive of my music. It really was so wonderful that I want them all to know how much I appreciate it.

It's amazing to look out and see the joy, the excitement in an audience halfway around the world from where you were born. There's nothing like when you first start playing a song and feeling the elation in that audience. It's truly special. I found myself so in tune with giving them everything I had in appreciation of their appreciation. It's genuine communication and that's what's so special about what I do. It proves what I've always believed that music crosses all borders and all cultures.

When you come off stage in Japan, they expect you to do an encore. It's a given that you will do at least one more song; that expectation is even stronger than it is here in America. It's like going through a gauntlet when you leave the stage and pass through the audience. Everybody wants to touch you. Everyone wants to hug you. It's amazing. I'm sure they do this with other artists, not just me. It's part of their culture. One special thing they did for me there was they made me a 50th anniversary cake, to celebrate my career in music. They appreciate the fact that you go all that way just to entertain them. One of my hopes is that I can one day tour all the Asian countries—maybe the Philippines, Korea, perhaps Macau.

The sound was magnificent in the Tokyo clubs where I played. The first day you go in there, you do a sound check and everything on stage is perfect, so the next time you go in there to play, the sound is the exact same. As a matter of fact, it's almost impossible to duplicate the sound they give you. In most places, when you're on stage, you're experiencing two kinds of sound: the audience and the band. When you're in some venues, you're getting more of the crowd because it's such a closed space. The band had a blast because of the quality in which we could hear ourselves play.

There's so much else about Japan that impressed and still impresses me. Let's start with the idea that there's no such thing as a dirty car in Japan. I don't care if it rained fifteen minutes ago, that car is immaculate.

The busses are immaculate; the trucks are immaculate. What's also interesting is the way the Japanese think about time. Everybody is on time. If you say you're going to be someplace at 10:30, you better be there at 10:30, as it's an affront to be late.

The other thing that's different is that nobody takes a tip. They simply won't take it. You attempt to, and they give it back to you. It's so different. And I have to mention the food. We had our own chef. He cooked us anything we wanted. It was all healthy food, which can be a true rarity on the road.

I've always believed you get back what you give. I learned that from my Swami, and in many ways, it's what I felt there in Tokyo. If you believe in energy exuding from your body, then the audience gets the message. They feel the energy. They feel the positive, uplifting energy you're conveying. That "feeling," to me at least, is primary in music. If you take music when it started and then you go through the opera period and then the classical period, you can't say it's getting any better.

One reason is so much of today's music is electronic. It's manufactured. It's an evolution, but I don't think you could say it's a positive evolution. The challenge is you don't want to sound like the old man, saying, "In my day, oh it was so much better." I just do my best to bring people to a place where they feel the music and experience the joy. That much hasn't changed from the time I was 25 to today, no matter where I'm playing. It's what I was put on this earth to do.

Today, I'm fortunate to work with people who also love to play music. Take my current band, "Felix Cavaliere's Rascals." Simply put, they are family. Expert musicians, incredibly talented people who play on the records of many other artists who you know. When I first moved to Nashville back in the eighties, I wanted to immediately connect to the music scene here. The first thing I did was go out and find the best players. In Nashville, you'll find great players on every street corner, but, as with the Rascals, I didn't want "great," I wanted "best." And I found them. It's interesting to consider how musicians find each other and what makes them stay together.

There have been a couple of changes, but this iteration of the band remains one of the finest I've had the pleasure of working beside. All talented, highly sought-after studio musicians and I'm happy to say that, when they're not playing on or producing others' records, they are performing with me on the road. Individually and collectively, they're magical, sharing the joy with me on stage every night we play.

On stage it's an absolute pleasure to introduce each member, encouraging them to take a bow. I thought it would be fun to do the same thing here:

Starting with our drummer, Vince Santoro, the soul of our groove who has been with me the longest:

When I heard that Liberty Devito was going to do a tour with Billy Joel and that Felix would be needing a drummer for some upcoming shows in 1999 it was one of those "drop what you're doing and make some calls" moments. I have looked back on that first rehearsal in Felix's basement and been ever so thankful it turned out that I'd be his singing drummer for more than 20 years! Playing alongside Felix is one of my most treasured professional experiences.

Of course, the music comes first but our friendship has also evolved over the years. Turns out Felix is a regular guy with a warm and engaging personality who treats everyone with humility. Am I lucky or what? The music is exactly how I grew up hearing it and Felix gives me the freedom to be myself within that structure. Being his sideman was something I could've only dreamed of. After all his success with the original band he treats us current members like WE are the Rascals! He hits the stage bursting with a confidence that is contagious to the rest of us and when the curtain falls we know we've done our best. The years have flown by but each show we play together is a fresh and honest expression from us all and Felix is a guy I'll follow as long as he wants to lead.

Looking over at Felix in his furry hat while visiting the Great Wall of China made me pause to consider how otherworldly a moment I was living.

My guitarist of more than 20 years is the incredibly talented and second longest tenured member of our band, Mike Severs:

My time as a member of Felix's band began in a very memorable way. It was New Year's Eve 2000 at the Rock & Roll Hall of Fame. We rang in the new millennium along with Wilson Pickett. It was a once in a lifetime "Midnight Hour," and a dream come true. Working with Felix since then on stage and in the recording studio has been the highlight of my career. Playing the rascals' hits that I loved for so long with the man who wrote and sang them is an amazing experience, but it doesn't end there. Felix is constantly learning, writing and evolving as a musician, singer, writer and human being. It has been an honor to be along for the ride.

On Bass is the versatile and gifted John Howard:

I've been playing with Felix in Felix Cavaliere's Rascals close to a decade now and the experience of performing on stage with him has been one of the true highlights of my musical life. If I had to say one thing about him, it would be that he is the joy of music personified. As a singer, a keyboardist, a songwriter and foremost as a friend, he captures and lives the reason that I started playing bass in the first place. Making music because you love it and want to share that essence of the music. The magic that happens when we get onstage and start a musical conversation between us - onstage and beyond, that runs throughout the entire show - starts and ends with that soulful voice, dynamic B3 organ, those timeless classic songs and the musical celebration as a whole that happens between Felix and the audience every single night. To me, there is one reason he does this and as I said above, it is simply because he loves it. He loves sharing that joy of the music and that connection with everyone in the audience. It isn't a money thing or an ego thing, just simply a love thing.

Going back to the beginning, my first experience playing bass with Felix's Rascals was in 2010 when I was asked along with a couple of my best friends on guitar and drums, to do a couple of stateside dates and then head off to Japan with Felix for a week of shows. One of my earliest and still best memories was that first sound check in Tokyo. There was a B3 brought in for Felix and he was testing it and trying out the sounds but he didn't look too thrilled. Then he just disappeared. I worked on my mix for a little while and wondered where he had gone. Then I noticed two feet sticking out from under the organ and walked around the front of it to see Felix kneeling underneath it with the access cover off and a screwdriver in his hand, adjusting some switches and holding court with the techs at the same time. He then slides out, plays a couple notes and with a big smile on his face proclaims "got it!". And we went on to have a great sound check and show. I knew right then that playing with Felix's Rascals was going to be special. And of course, the Hammond sounded great after that, so great in fact that it had to be shipped to every show with us until we left Japan

There are so many memorable moments onstage with Felix that it's really hard to come up with singular highlights but another one does come to mind. A few years back (around 2016-17), we were doing a multi-artist show in Palm Desert called the Warburton, headed by the actor Patrick Warburton in order to raise funds for St Jude. Our band Sixwire is the house band for this event every year. We had been hoping to get Felix on the show for a while but scheduling can be a bear. Coincidentally, Felix had a show booked in Indio the same night as the Warburton that year, so I asked Felix if he would want to come straight over from that show and be a surprise guest on the Warburton show afterward. Of course, he said yes, and mind you, this is a benefit and it was going to be logistically difficult but that's just how he is, Felix loves making music and he has always been there to help out St Jude. As the show was gearing up for the end of the night, after several artists had performed, it is announced to "welcome surprise guest Felix Cavaliere of the Rascals!" And Felix just walks up to his keyboard without any sound check or preparation and proceeds to blow the doors down. I will always have this vivid memory of looking from my left to right onstage and seeing Skunk Baxter of the Doobies / Steely Dan, Mike Mills of REM & Tommy Thayer of KISS joining us onstage with their guitars on, and at the same time Alice Cooper is standing there watching the show side stage with a massive smile on his face. It turns out Felix was a big influence on all of them and they wanted to share in this moment with him. And at that moment, I could literally see the power and the influence that Felix and his music has had on so many artists from such varied musical worlds. Thinking about that reminds me of a phrase that Felix likes to say onstage, "just let the music be your guide". From my viewpoint of Felix, I'd say that is a pretty good guide.

On Keyboards is the energic and funny Benny Harrison:

My time with Felix....well it goes back to 1966 when my father took me to see the BEATLES at Shea Stadium. I had just seen the Rascals at a Murry the K music extravaganza that he threw at the RKO Theatre on east 58th street. It was the first time The Who/Cream/ came to America. Mitch Ryder and the Detroit Wheels, Wilson Pickett, with Buddy Miles on drums, Al Kooper...great lineup.... then The Young Rascals came on and blew a hole in the room. I was mind fucked! Forward to 1966 at Shea. My dad and I had nosebleed seats so I worked my way down to the dugout where I thought they would be coming out and there was Felix signing autographs in the same shirt and hat he wore on the Collections Album cover.

Having played with Felix since 2018, besides the musicality and the songs, my favorite times are hearing the stories he tells about the Rascal Days...funny stuff. One that comes to mind, is when they were coming back from Canada to the states and some fan slipped Eddie some joints in his bag. Eddie had to get searched at the border and didn't want to take of his pants for a body search. He kept saying to the inspector that he felt uncomfortable about getting down to his skivvies. Inspector insisted.... his boxer's that he was wearing said BLOW ME! There are always funny stories he shares.

The great rush for me is to be part of Felix's present musical reality and being part of his new recording. Felix's music is a big part of my DNA. We complement each other both musically and vocally. I had mentioned that to Felix; I thought it was because I knew his style so well and he said No, Ben. It's simpatico. I understand where he comes from and I am fortunate to have him as not only my boss, but my mentor and my friend. I feel Felix is in the same class as Fagan and Becker, Michael McDonald....all of us who have been influenced by his songs and style. He truly invented the Blue-Eyed Soul genre. Those songs are timeless.

BTW, I pre-ordered the book.

I'd be remiss if I didn't mention Mark Prentice. Mark toured with me as a valued member for years.

"I first saw Felix with the Young Rascals just after my 13th birthday and it changed my life forever. The odds on that night that I would ever even meet those guys, much less play music and become friends with them were right at zero.

Fast forward many years and my career crossed paths with Felix in 1997 and we worked together playing bass for the better part of 18 years. This included literally traveling around the world together.

From the moment I first heard him sing and the moment I first stood on a stage with him until this very day, Felix's unique talent continues to blow me away. He is absolutely among the best soul singers in the world, still delivering these definitive songs in their original keys while adding creativity, energy and originality to every performance.

We've shared the stage in about every imaginable circumstance from the sublime to the ridiculous but it was always a thrill and an honor to play this timeless music with this iconic singer.

I treasure the friendship we have, the music we've made on stage and in the studio and the many hilarious stories and laughs we've had along the way."

All the best,

MP

My longtime Production manager, Mike Malfeasi, another Italian has done a brilliant job of keeping our sound grooving:

We spent 10 minutes or so talking about good music, but the next half hour was all about food. Felix loves good food. I love good food. We had an immediate connection.

Step back to 1967. I'm a sophomore in high school and I have a ticket to see The Rascals in the auditorium. I was absolutely blown away with the soulful stuff I had never heard before. And as a drummer, Dino blew my mind. I was forever changed after that show.

Fast forward. I got the gig! I am blessed to work with this man and all of Team Felix for the last six years. Here we are in the challenging early 2020s and Felix continues to keep his music relevant and alive, engaging audiences everywhere, singing his heart out every night and expressing his message of love for the timeless music he shares with everyone. His desire to spread the joy of music to all is intoxicating and it lifts your spirits, allowing you to forget any of your troubles for a while. Anyone who experiences one of his live shows leaves feeling part of a family. I am privileged to be a small part of that family, especially when his wife, Donna, makes meatballs that rival my Grandma Capalone's meatballs circa 1963.

Cent'anni! (Italian for 100 Years!)

I'm really grateful to have such talented and professional musicians around me all the time touring all over the United States and the world. They simply match my passion and love of playing before a crowd. We've had so many adventures together on the road, probably more than I can remember, but I'm reminded every so often of the fun that comes from playing and challenging yourself on stage every night.

There are many other tremendous musicians who perform with us from time to time: the great Lance Hoppen, bass player from the band Orleans. Steve Hornbeak, Chuck Tilley, Jimmy Keneally, and Steve Mandille, just to name a few.

With Felix Cavaliere's Rascals," we had a night when we were playing in Georgia, outside Atlanta, opening for the Beach Boys. The company providing the main PA system was late in setting everything up, so soundchecks got pushed back. We ended up just basically plugging in our instruments and playing. Everybody except us was worried about the fact there was no sound check. That night, Mike Severs remembers, was like being back in 1966. When we came off stage, none of us knew how it sounded, so Mike asked his wife, who said, "You guys were amazing." She thought we never sounded better. Sometimes you just got to go out and play. That was one of those nights that harkened back to the Rascals of yesteryear—we just went out and played.

That's why people come to shows—to hear something special, something that they can't hear by staying home and playing the records. It's the way I learned at Atlantic records, make the music front and center and don't be afraid to improvise. After a half-century, I've pretty much gotten used to improvising on the spot. If the sound isn't always perfect, so what? I'll deal with whatever the problem is later; it's not the audience's problem. We're there to entertain, to perform, to put smiles on people's faces. That's just what we do. It's sad that all artists don't feel that way. As I've said previously, some artists are just jerks. They take their frustrations out on stage. I've never done that. When you're a pro, you get through it.

There's obviously so much that goes into performance, and of course travel is among the most demanding. Preparation is key, but sometimes it's just a matter of getting there. There are times where the routing from one show to another involves thousands of miles making it impossible to do by bus. These days we mostly travel separately by air, renting cars and vans in the town or city we're playing.

I'll usually fly out to a show the day before with my road manager. The others fly out together from Nashville. Then, we all meet up the next morning, the day of the show, to go over our set list and such. It runs like a fine-tuned engine and that makes my role so much easier, which always adds to a more pleasurable experience for all of us.

One of the coolest things with my current band is the interaction between us, or what John Howard, my bass player, calls the musical "conversation" that goes on. He describes it as being like a river: "You never know where the water's going to go. You never quite know what you might play on a given night, but you know it's going to be fun." If some old song just occurs to me, I'll launch into it and the guys will follow. That's where the fun comes in and is probably another reason why the "Once Upon a Dream" show never quite worked for me. I'm a musician, a creator; I want to jam, feed off the crowd, and create in the moment.

That same creative impulse has led me in a number of directions since the Rascals. One of them began in 1988 when I met Chris Clouser, who has become a lifelong friend. At the time, he was the CEO of Bell-Atlantic. We met when I did a show in Virginia, at a place called Wolf Trap, a big venue where a lot of famous artists play. Back then, I didn't have a manager, so I was kind of adrift, you might say. Well, Chris comes up and talks to me after the show. It was around the time of the election, the one George HW Bush won. So, here's this gentleman who approaches me and says, "all of you rock guys used to be about the hippie generation, talking about how everything was going to change for the better. What happened?"

His proposed solution was to set up a kind of apolitical, non-denominational effort to get out the vote. He invited Jimmy Carter, Gerald Ford, and a lot of present and former politicians, to try to promote some kind of sanity in the political process. Putting his money where his mouth is, he paid me six figures to play a show that would bring people together around a common cause. Money or not, this was right up my alley, although I appreciated the intent behind it, and, at that time, the money was certainly useful, the concept was such that I would have performed without fee because I believed in it.

Chris went on to work for Sprint in a management capacity and eventually ended up as the CEO of Northwest Airlines. That's when my entry into doing commercials began. Chris loved R&B music and had this idea that we could integrate it into a television commercial campaign for the airline. I suddenly went to work for a major corporation because it was what Chris wanted done and he was in charge, so we got to do it. It was a blast. Northwest had people write the scripts and my role was to simulate the songs of a lot of major, historic R&B artists. I got to sing with people like Mavis Staples and Isaac Hayes—giants whom I'd always admired. Good work if you can find it and I did. I was able to go and do the commercials in places like Memphis and Detroit, among the funkiest cities of all time.

Honestly, it doesn't matter a lot to me where I'm playing or what I'm playing, as long as it puts a smile on people's faces. Who's to say those commercials didn't make somebody's day just as much as any song of mine they might hear on the radio? You never fully know what will make a difference in others' lives. I sang at a benefit show in California awhile back for St. Jude's Hospital with Alice Cooper. It put such big smiles on the kids' faces and, in that situation, those kids and their families could certainly use something to smile about.

And then, there was Alice Cooper. You might not think I'd have a lot in common with a performer who uses guillotines among his many crazy antics on stage, but the fact is he's an incredibly kind, down-to-earth humanitarian for whom I greatly admire. I stayed around to watch his set from the wings and heard him say that he was "honored" to see me off-stage watching him play. Musicians are musicians. We have a special bond, no matter the differences within our performances.

One of the more memorable shows I've done as a solo act was at a school in Massachusetts. It was a benefit gala for the school. What made it different was that all the kids in the school were blind. They weren't just there to listen, either. They sang and played with me on "Lonely Too Long" and "Good Lovin." Talk about special! One of the kids, a young man as I recall, played fiddle on the songs. I'd never heard a fiddle on "Good Lovin'" or even thought about it, but it certainly added to the performance. These kids were so excited, so tuned in. It proves that you don't have to see to feel the music; you only need a heart.

Time after time, when I've had the opportunity to play with young people it's been special. Back in 2014, I was convinced by my manager that I should do a holiday album. I was skeptical. Everybody has a holiday album, right? But we decided to move forward with the idea of doing a few cover songs and adding in a little Christmas music. We figured we'd redo some of the classic songs from Phil Spector's Christmas album, which I'd listened to repeatedly as a kid. It was supposed to be a modest little project, but turned into something much bigger, taking longer to produce than we intended and resulted in a tour that involved not only me and my band but a high school choir performing with us in most of the cities we played.

That was something I wasn't really used to, and on the first few dates, it made me a little nervous, to be honest with you. It wasn't because I was nervous for me, but for the kids. They'd rehearse long before we'd arrive, and we'd only have a limited time to rehearse together on the day of the show. I wanted it to be right for them, and for the most part, it went well. Their energy, enthusiasm, and talent just made it something different from everything else we do on the road. It created a kind of spark that I started to look forward to each night. Most nights we finished with all the kids on stage at the end for an encore. It was very, very memorable. I'm confident it's something special that those kids and their parents will always remember and I'm proud to have been a part of it.

When you talk about the bond that music creates it's impossible for me not to talk about Billy Joel. I've played with Billy at least four or five times, including near my home in Nashville, on Long Island, and in Hartford. He's a phenomenal musician and has been nothing but kind to me, in ways that I'll describe later. I played with him a couple of times at Madison Square Garden, once with Gene joining in, and we all did "Good Lovin.'" I was in town with my band playing B.B. King's club when my daughter Lisa and my wife, Donna, wanted me to go over and play with Billy. To tell you the truth, I was tired that night, but once I got out on stage, the energy was infectious.

Playing with Billy Joel over the years points out something else that sometimes, in the middle of all the travel and the business side of music you might overlook. I have to say that when you're in this business you never really know who you influence. You have a better shot at naming those who influenced you. Well, Billy is one of those gents who has talked about how much I influenced him as a kid growing up on Long Island. Maybe it's because we were both in our teens and there weren't a lot of keyboard players doing rock in those days. Jerry Lee Lewis on piano doing the boogie-woogie stuff was one, but there weren't a lot. Even fewer were playing organ. As my friend Tommy James puts it, "an organ was something you had in your living room and you polished it, you didn't play it."

Billy heard all those Rascals' records and apparently got something from them. That night in Madison Square Garden in 2016, he told the audience the Rascals were the best rock and roll group he'd ever heard. Those two words—the best—really connect with me. It takes a little while for that to sink in, partially because there have been so many great rock and roll bands, but it made me think about Eddie, Gene, and Dino, being in our twenties, writing and producing music that lasts. That's special, and to have someone like Billy Joel recognize that and ask you up on stage to play only adds to how truly special it really is.

It's the same with an artist like Paul Shaffer, who is kind to say that seeing me for the first time on "Hullabaloo" back in the '60s, had a profound and lasting influence on him. Paul, of course, was the long-time bandleader on the "David Letterman Show" and a wonderful person who I've gotten to know well over the past few years. Back on "Letterman," there came a time when people started sitting in with the band and I certainly took advantage of such an opportunity. Paul has told people that, as far as using the Hammond organ in soul and rock music, I was the pioneer, the "template," he called it. That's something else of which I'm very proud. On the other hand, he jokingly adds that thanks to me, musicians like him who played the Hammond got to lug around these huge pieces of furniture to gigs!

Paul and I have shared other significant moments, like the Atlantic Records anniversary concert at the old Madison Square Garden. Led Zeppelin closed that night, but we, the Rascals were on just before them and used Paul's band as the rhythm section backing us. And, when I received the Harry Chapin Humanitarian Award from the World Hunger Association (about which I'll speak a little later), Paul presented it to me.

Paul also presented me into the Musician's Hall of Fame. In addition, we played an unplugged set together. I have to say that it's pretty cool when you elicit respect from somebody like Paul, who says you really impacted his life in a positive way.

The last few years have brought me back to some of the most joyous places I've ever known and some of the best memories I've had the privilege to share with others. In late 2016 and early 2017, I played with my band in Hawaii, a wonderful experience that brought back amazing memories. In the Rascals days, we had such a tremendous time there, as

I've mentioned, and playing there again so many years later brought so much of that back. When I think of it today, I remember all those great times with our families and other artists, the people who supported us, like Tom Moffat, a radio station owner, promoter, and an absolutely wonderful human being who was principally responsible for making us famous on the islands.

As an illustration of just how much I love Hawaii and its people, in 2017 I played a show on a Friday night in Las Vegas, and right after the show took a red eye to Maui to do a show the following evening. Was it tiring? Absolutely. Was it worth it? Totally. "Ohana." "Family." We were like family to our fans and the people we knew there. And, in the end, family is what really stands out; that's what's truly important, not gold records, halls of fame, accolades, or awards. It's family. It's how I was raised, and what I spent a lifetime searching to find after my mother's untimely passing. It's what I thought I found and lost with the Rascals. Most importantly, it's what I'm grateful to have found again, beginning with my beautiful wife, Donna.

She and I met through a mutual friend named Linda, who called me one afternoon and wanted me to meet her friend at a nearby Starbucks. Donna wasn't anxious. She had just been out shopping in the heat and didn't feel comfortable meeting someone new. She tells the story better than I do, so I'll use mostly her own words to convey that first meeting. I'll never forget it and I doubt she will either, but only our closest friends, some of whom were there around the time, know the whole story.

I was watching a Master's Tournament on TV and Tiger Woods was in a playoff. It was a sudden death situation. So, I wasn't anxious to leave when my friend Linda phoned to invite me out. I was glued to the TV set. Then, along came what must have been a divine intervention.

The sudden death was over in minutes; I switched off the set and went out to meet Linda and get introduced to Donna. We had a really good conversation, talking about everything, from books to politics. So, here I am with a woman who I found interesting, but she had no clue who I was.

That might have been a good thing. "We talked about life, about spirituality, just about everything except music, nothing about music," is how Donna remembers it. And that, too, was probably a good thing, given that her ex-husband was in the music business. Donna recalls I looked at my watch and said I had to go to keep a dinner appointment. "So, this very nice man suddenly gets up and very chivalrously thanks me for the conversation we'd just had," Donna recalls about that first interaction.

I didn't get very far down the street before I kind of hit myself on the side of the head and turned the car around. It hit me. What was I thinking? Here's this lovely, smart woman and I just left her there at a table so I could go off to this dinner with three guys. It didn't make sense. Donna and Linda stayed to finish their coffee when all of a sudden, they saw a car backing straight up to the table, right there on the sidewalk. I got out and the first thing Donna remembers me saying was, 'What am I doing? I'd like to invite you to dinner, both of you." Fortunately, for me, both ladies accepted.

We just talked and talked. Donna's recollection is that I said something along the lines of "If you don't mind, can I give you a call next week?" And that's how it began. I gave her a call and asked if she'd like to join me for dinner at the Brentwood Country Club. She accepted. What she didn't know was that her life around the music business was about to begin again. "It was a beautiful place, but I remember thinking it was kind of odd like there were a lot of people there, not exactly like it was an intimate setting, and then I noticed there was a whole stage set up, with lights and sound," Donna remembers. "Then, at one point, this man who I barely knew, named Felix, said 'I'm sorry. I have to go. I'll be back.' Just like that, the lights went down in the room, the stage lights came up, and he ran on stage and the band started doing "It's a Beautiful Morning."

At that point, Donna says it suddenly hit her that I was "that guy" from the record. "I just didn't believe it was him," she says to this day. "It was just such a surprise. From that point forward, we've almost never been out of each other's sight." That was 2005; in 2014, Donna and I formalized our relationship by getting married. Actually, it was the third time we got married— the first two were what I'd term "spiritual marriages." The first performed by a Tibetan monk, the second by a Swami, and then the most recent—the legal one, I guess you'd call it—by a Justice of the Peace in nearby Franklin, Tennessee.

It wasn't my first wedding, and neither was it Donna's. She once was married to a man in the music business and, for a time, worked in it herself, not as a performer, but as the right-hand person to some pretty big artists like Waylon Jennings, Johnny Cash, and Willie Nelson—especially during the period when they were together with Kris Kristofferson as "The Highwaymen." Like me, she saw a lot of the road and a lot of the stuff that goes on backstage, all of which isn't pretty, not by a long shot. Donna connects with the music, but says Waylon once told her, "Oh, Donna, you poor thing. You're a musician without an instrument," because she loves to sing, but doesn't have the voice. But, for me, she brings a different kind of voice, one that I love, need, and cherish in my everyday life.

Given my own track record in life and love, not to mention marriage, what I now have with Donna is really remarkable and I'm thankful for it. One of the reasons we get along so well is that she's not what I would call a "civilian." Donna's work with the Highwaymen is one part of her past connection to the music business and today she still does design work for country artists like Allan Jackson and Garth Brooks. Why is that important to our ability to connect? Because the road is a beast of its own. It really isn't like anything most people imagine. It's a job, like any other job; it has its conditions, it has its perks, and it has its negatives. You have to be aware of that, especially when it comes to having your husband away so much. Not to mention, a lot of wives get ticked off when other women come up and want to hug and kiss you. It's not easy having that not so understanding set of eyes locked onto you. Fans are fans. I know, because I'm often a fan myself. I get it. I'm not about to push someone away. That's not who I am. So, it takes a special person to understand what the road is like, and Donna does. She's been there.

I'm so proud of all my kids and am so grateful that they are in my and Donna's lives. Christina is my middle child. I was away a lot when she was growing up, but Christina really grew into a very self-aware child. She's an example of how much kids remember from their youth. Back then, I lived in Danbury, Connecticut, and I've mentioned how my dear friend, Laura Nyro, was a neighbor. Christina remembers staying with Laura frequently while growing up. She calls those the "best years" of her childhood and says Laura was like another mother to her. Christina's recollection is of music always playing and "kind of being aware" by the age of three that her father didn't exactly have a traditional job.

That manifested itself a lot over the course of the years in my relationship with all my kids. My parents were in "normal" professions: dentistry and pharmacy. Here I am, their kid, with kids of my own, running all around the country and all around the world playing rock and roll night after night, week after week. It can't help but take its toll, but I think each of the kids, in their own way, have had some fun with it, too. A few years ago, after finding an old clip of me singing "You Better Run" on YouTube, Christina wrote on her Facebook page:

This was another one of those times in my life (where I was SUPER excited about my Daddy) The Dr Pepper commercial came out... right around the time that

BIG Chill took off… and I am pretty sure this is when I realized that My Dad was a ROCKSTAR

When I was home, I tried to make life as "normal" as possible. I used to take Christina with me shopping, usually, as she remembers it, for hand-made leather goods in those days, not to mention making my regular trips to music stores. I've always been someone who taps into the latest "thing," especially technology, so I'd take Christina along to check out what was new and different. Among her fondest memories of those days is that I bought her a Sony Walkman, her first one, as well as her first CD. One of the great things back then is that there weren't any paparazzi following us, which is so different from today when rock stars and their kids go out. It was a very different time and, thank God, since Danbury is a small town, and it would have been difficult to do everyday things without having your kids getting put in the spotlight.

It probably seems like a small thing to most people, but Christina recalls that when I was home, and that wasn't a lot, I'd sit down and read the newspaper with her. We'd always have a conversation about what was going on in the world, which is something I still do; I keep up with current events and enjoy talking about the news of the day. Christina says that I "always try to learn and evolve" and I hope I always will. On the other hand, my middle daughter calls me "an eternal hippie," which I probably am. Most of all, she has come to believe she and I share this in common: "He (meaning me) was the rebel in his family. I'm the rebel in my family. We had no choice but to hang out."

Where I used to have some pretty quiet times with Christina, the opposite was the case with the twins—Laura and Aria. I didn't know this, but Christina's insight is interesting—that Aria and Laura were always "loud" growing up. I think, like they say about twins in general, they shared and still share a special bond. They certainly are special to me; that's for sure. They're each different but equally special.

Christina has a bachelor's degree from Middle Tennessee State University. She decided, after raising two children, to go into restaurant management. Her children, Malia and Leo, are 23 and 20 as I write. Leo was a phenomenal athlete, a wrestler and is now making his way in the business world, and Malia is a talented dancer who has become a teacher.

I call Laura "my student." She's very much a career person, an architect, with a master's degree from Parsons School of Design in New York and a bachelor's degree from Emerson College in Boston.

Aria is the singer. I mean all my kids can sing, but Aria is the one who pursued it as a career and she's unbelievable. She's also too nice a kid to be in the music business. I mentioned in the last chapter that she sang on one of my solo albums and she has also appeared with me singing on stage. She's so well named. It is, of course, a musical name, coming from opera, which is especially appropriate for a musician's daughter.

When I first heard her sing on stage, she blew everybody away, me included. Honestly, I cry every time I hear her. These days she sings in church as a head cantor and is still writing and recording new songs. I am very glad that she decided to become a mother and raise a family.

I am also blessed with two more grandchildren, Aria's two girls, Gemma, at this writing age 8, and Gia, 6.

That's a part of my life that Donna has shared so fully. Even before we were married, she stepped right into the lives of my kids and grandkids, especially with Aria's children. She really has been pretty much a mother to all the kids and spends so much time with the grandchildren. I think the same thing happens with grandchildren as occurs with children. You're close to them until they become teenagers and then it becomes a little harder as they begin to spread their wings and begin discovering their impact upon life, as they should. I certainly hope they recognize how proud of them I am, and how thankful I am that they're all living so close to me here in Nashville, a place I dragged all my kids to over 20 years ago

It's where they were raised and went to school, and now it's where they choose to live and raise their own families. I was once asked if I thought I'm a better grandfather than I was a father. I can't really say that. I think it's too soon. I think most of us, when we're young, are working hard at whatever we do and tend to overdo with our grandchildren, maybe to make up for missing a lot of events with our kids. I messed up a lot in the beginning and I hope I've somewhat made up for it.

Like most of us, as we age, I'd like to think I've learned a few things that might make me at least slightly better at relationships today than I was in the past. I'm not the best judge of that, but if you know the whole story, I think you might agree, dating back to my first relationship, which resulted in the first two of my five children. Her name is Ruby Toy, the beautiful young lady who dragged me to the Metropole to watch Dino play drums through the window—a moment in time captured in "Once Upon a Dream." Our relationship produced two children, a son, Joseph, and a daughter, Lisa.

My first wife, Theresa, and I were married in 1980. Theresa blessed me with Christina, Laura, and Aria before our divorce in 2004. Theresa was a great mom to our daughters, no question about it. She had her own demons, being the child of an alcoholic. I found out along the way in our marriage just how bad having an alcoholic parent can screw up a child and her siblings. Theresa tried hard to escape her childhood; she so wanted to be a part of Swamiji's philosophy and really, for a time, got into it. She was very spiritual, but couldn't, in the long run, take care of herself and her health. She became diabetic and never was able to fully control the disease. She passed away in 2014. I will always say she was a wonderful mother, and after the dust settled from our divorce, we became close friends and remained that way right up to her passing.

That same year, 2014, I suffered another tremendous loss. My daughter, Lisa, passed away from cancer. Remember it was that fateful phone call from Lisa that led to the Kristin Carr benefit concert that initially reunited the Rascals. Lisa lost her own battle with cancer, and it was devastating. She was a special kid, so beautiful and so loved. Even when it was obvious toward the end that she wouldn't survive, she kept fighting, always smiling and always having a sense of humor. Lisa had her mother's Chinese smarts; she was a really good businesswoman, and so much more.

One of Lisa's favorite things to say about our relationship was, "I inherited your nose and your lawsuits!" The latter refers to how, when the Rascals lawsuits were ongoing, she also was involved in lawsuits relating to the partners in her limo company. She could joke about that because she never let things get her down, and that quality inspired so many others. When she passed, it was unbelievable the number of stars who came to the funeral. It went on for like three days and you've never seen so many flowers. Paul McCartney sent some; so did the members of U-2. Billy Joel took on many of the particulars, from food to finance and most everything in between. Flowers are certainly special because of the thought, the recognition they represent. And, yet for some special reasoning, that wasn't quite enough for Billy. He donated his time and energy along with his generosity, and that's simply a show of love that I'll always hold dear to my heart. Thank you, my friend!!

To this day, Lisa's presence is always with me and seems to shine brightest backstage wherever I play, especially in the venues where she was so well known. It's a tribute to her legacy, how many people she touched in her life, and how loved she was. The last time I played Madison Square Garden with Billy Joel, I was inundated with well-wishers who went out of their way to express their love for Lisa, in addition to their support for me. "We want you to know you're family. Anything you need." These were just a few of the well wishes I received that evening. Her life had a profound impact on people. It still does.

Lisa, my love, there's not a day that passes where my heart doesn't ache, and my soul doesn't smile within your memory.

We all experience setbacks in life, hard, seemingly crushing times: spiritually, physically, and emotionally. We take our hits and lean on our loved ones along with our faith as well as other powerful lessons to get us through. I had a fire ravage through my home in 2001. Everything was lost, including the Baldwin piano from my parent's living room in Pelham. They bought a Baldwin because, although a large financial sacrifice at the time, it wasn't as steep as a Steinway. That piano held great significance because it had shared my mother's hands and was the instrument on which many of the Rascals' songs were written. Sure, it had memories for me, but so did a lot of things that I'll never see again: family photos, gold records, and so much more. It was, for a time, pretty devastating to me. That is until I did a show at the Kentucky Derby and learned that the gentleman who had brought the band and me in had lost his grandchildren in a fire. There's tragedy, and then there's tragedy!

If nothing else does, when you think about that, it has to make you grateful, even if you can't completely understand why some things happen in your life that may appear to be beyond your control. Some of those are things that I still don't get, but I try hard to understand.

When you've been through a life spent in rock and roll and come out alive on the other side, that's pretty much something for which you have to be grateful. I've always felt like there's been someone or something looking out for me. I believe strongly in that because I've almost died several times and, yet I'm still here. I've had some pretty precarious situations. Once I was in Greenwich Village, and I went to get out of the car because I was late for an appointment. The door jammed, so I couldn't get out. Thank God I couldn't. A car sped by no more than three or four inches from my car; if I had been able to open that door, I wouldn't be here. I'm certain it's no coincidence that the name "Felix" translates from Latin to "lucky and successful."

There have been so many "lucky" milestones in my life since the Rascals disbanded. In 2010, I reached a major one that brought me full circle back to where it all began in Pelham Manor. I got a call to receive an award at my old high school, where I graduated in 1960. In addition to the award itself, I got a chance to play for the kids and the faculty of Pelham Manor High in the school's auditorium. It was great on so many levels. It was just me, the students, and an upright piano. No band. No amplification. No stage lights. Just me and my future fellow alum.

That day I played "Whole Lot of Shakin Goin On" by Jerry Lee Lewis and "What'd I Say" by Ray Charles in addition to "Good Lovin." Those hugely impactful songs of my day that I decided to share with the kids of today, many of whom clapped and sang along, which made it all the more special. That afternoon brought me back to my parent's living room and all the friends who supported us when we played the dances, the roller rinks, the proms, you name it. It began with my introduction to rock and roll while in line right here at this very school.

It really was quite an experience. I couldn't believe how much things at my old school had changed, including the addition of so many Italian families in comparison to the two or three when we moved to Pelham, there were just a couple of Italian families. I also immediately noticed that most of the staff at the school today appeared more diverse, coming from different backgrounds. That really jumped out at me. A lot of memories came back.

My childhood home was located right across the street from the school, and that's where I learned to play classical music and the Rascals first practiced as a band. As a kid, I could see the school from my bedroom window and here I was playing in the very same auditorium where I had played in so many talent shows as a student. It's where I had performed my talent show-winning routine, doing impressions of Jerry Lee Lewis and Little Richard; it's also where I had brought in a Doo-wop group and where we won first place in the school competition. Being back there was really moving.

It came back to me how, during my student days, the school would bring in these famous classical musicians. So, here I am getting an award in a room where, as a boy, I used to spend time being in awe of the people who played classical music there. It was like you go into a place in your memory where recollection springs to a peak, and memories grow sound and seemingly color. I've been all over the world, but this was different.

This was home. My sister, Fran, came and I felt so honored. It's hard to describe all my feelings surrounding that day, but I think that, as with so many things in my life, gratitude is at the core of the experience.

What a journey I had from there, in Pelham Manor, to the Rock and Roll Hall of Fame, not to mention all the other honors for which I am grateful, many of which mean more to me than I'm able to fathom. I've been privileged to be recognized by so many Italian American organizations around the country, which have filled me with such pride knowing how proud my parents would be to see me recognized in such a way.

You know, I never changed my name, though there was a lot of pressure in the record business to do so in those days. The record companies always wanted easy names to remember and pronounce—but I insisted on always being Felix Cavaliere because I'm proud of my family name and the heritage it represents. If you come from an Italian or Mediterranean heritage, you know what I mean, but even if you don't, I'm certain you know what it's like to stand up and be proud of whatever culture or ethnicity you celebrate. It's something that was passed on to you by your parents—and, if your parents are no longer with you, there's even more serenity in knowing how proud they would be.

While I return to my roots in New York several times a year, my life today really is in Nashville. When you're a New Yorker, I don't know that you're ever really at home anywhere else, but Nashville has been a good place for me, Donna, my kids, and grandchildren. It's really like my first home, now. It really is the Music City of the world. When I first came down here in the 1980s, I tried to be part of it—the country music scene. I just never could get into it. You know what, Johnny Cash is in the Rock and Roll Hall of Fame, I'm in the Rock and Roll Hall of Fame, so there should be some similarities between what he did and what I do, don't you think? Well, there were similarities at one time, but not since the direction country music has recently taken.

Everybody wonders about country's resurgence in popularity. Here's the way I see it. It's familiarity. I really believe that today's country music was created by what's going on in Hip-Hop music. What do I mean by that? It's simple. Country has become like the alternative to a kind of music that conservatives can't understand and don't want to. That's what I mean by familiarity. It's the same old themes, but now they're sung by really white, really good-looking people. The audience is young females as much as guys with big trucks—and no wonder. Take a look at some of these guys who look more like Chippendale dancers than musicians. And there's a "twang."

Today's Nashville has become a major metropolis. It boggles my mind how many people have moved here in the last few years. It ain't your grandaddy's Nashville anymore. One of the leading convention cities in America, everything about Nashville has become huge. It's crowded and everywhere you look you see construction cranes, buildings going up, and apartments being built. As far as the music goes, I do believe there's still an energy that exists and that's what I continue to like about it. I will add, however, that my politics clearly don't fit in.

To me, you can't separate your politics from how you live your life. What I learned from Swamiji really influences everything I do and the way I interact with others. To start with, ego is something you have to conquer; that's one of the primary lessons he taught me. Paalitha is the name I took during my studies with the guru in order to separate me from my past life and my ego. I can see that so many of the troubles I've had in my life, ranging from the breakup of the band, the lawsuits, all that really relates to one central thing: ego.

We could probably go the rest of our lives and see that ego is there everywhere; every time there's a problem, it's that. It's not a "band" story; it's a human story. It's universal. It applies to everybody's lives. We have to think of the greater good. Once we overcome ego, we can move forward to a higher level in this life. That's really what I want my message to be, and I hope it has come across. Get rid of ego and you become part of the universal truth and everything works out the way it's supposed to work out. Instead of "my" way, "your" way, "his" way, or "her" way, try to think of paths that lead us closer to "our way," toward connecting us to our common humanity.

"My motivation of self-interest, ulterior motives can give way to pure acts of friendship, leading to unconditional love and giving." That comes from a practice in the Jewish tradition of, every day, picking a card to read that contains some truth, something to help remind you of what's really important in life. I regularly go through these cards and pull out one that has relevance to my daily life. Here's another one that really gets across what I believe: "When I take myself out of the way, I create a space for true and loving friends, joy and fulfillment."

If there's anything I want to get across, it's that. It's what I believe and what I got from this great man, Swami Satchidananda, whose teachings, as I've said, still inform my life. He was a man who received tons of accolades from popes, presidents, leaders like Nelson Mandela, and yet he maintained his humility. That's the way I've always strived to be and how I'd like to one day be remembered.

One of the more recent honors I've received kind of reflects that philosophy. The late singer/songwriter Harry Chapin, who had hit records with "Cat's in the Cradle" and "Taxi," has an award named after him that recognizes achievements in humanitarian causes. I got a call in 2015 that I was going to receive what's called the "Harry Chapin Legacy Award." At the time I didn't really know what that was all about, but I've since learned that it recognizes those who give of their time and talent to support various social causes. Harry himself was an early advocate for world hunger charities, through a non-profit organization he founded called "Why Hunger." There was a big gala that summer in New York that included a lot of other musicians, Harry's daughters, and his brother Tom Chapin. It was really special. Paul Shaffer introduced me and I was asked to speak. In the spirit of that night, here's what I said:

I know that music transcends all boundaries. We work in countries that have major language barriers; they do not understand what we say, but they feel what we say. As part of my show, in the very last segment I do 'People Got to Be Free,' which I'm very proud to say in those days was a No. 1 hit in places that were oppressed all over the world. I'm talking about, in those days, Hong Kong, we're talking about Berlin, we're talking about South Africa. People have responded to the message and the energy that comes along when you talk about things such as freedom, whether it be as a social cause, as a political cause, or just as a mental, kind of like 'Leave me alone' cause… I always felt that music was very healing, and that's what I was supposed to be doing.

Shortly after that, I had a reporter for a newspaper in Colorado, where I was about to appear, ask me about that night and about musicians standing up for social justice, like the Rascals did when we took a stand on segregation, insisting black acts open for us. She asked me if there was a different attitude back then towards musicians—or any artists, for that matter—speaking out against societal injustice. I told her I thought there was, and I really believe there is to this day. I told her that the perfect example is John Lennon and what he was trying to do with Yoko. It wasn't necessary for us, the Rascals, to do that, but it was important for us to do that, to take a cause, whatever that might be, and just kind of herald it and try to tell people, "Look, in case you want to know where we stand, this is where we stand. "Today, I feel like people avoid that because they don't want to alienate the other sides of the argument. That wasn't the case then; artists like us actively campaigned for people, went out on the road, and devoted our time and talents to our beliefs. We were fully involved. As time went on, musicians began to realize that music is a business. However, even though it's a business, I've always felt that music should fill a purpose in people's lives. That purpose might change over time, but it still should have purpose; if you're an artist of any kind, purpose and principle should guide you beyond fame or fortune.

Look, I know I'm always going to be associated with that time in my life when I was with the Rascals, but I also know there's so much more to my life than those seven years. They amount to about only seven years out of the seventy-eight I've been on the planet—about 10 per cent of my life. It's almost ridiculous to identify myself solely with that era. It can't dictate my life. I need to keep moving forward, not looking back. And there's so much more to experience, so many more challenges to meet. The great thing about my "job" is there's always the next chapter to open, the next challenge that makes you look forward.

I'm sure we've all told our children; find a job you love to do. Let's face it; there are a lot of people who go to work every day and they're absolutely miserable. That's sad. If you're not one of those people, you're lucky. Be grateful because you're blessed. Despite all the problems, the destruction of the band, the ego battles, the lost money, all of it, I want you to know I love what I do and that's what keeps me going.

What also keeps me going is that I have a great team. They're all great, great people, not just from a business perspective, but from a personal one. They're all giving, loving people. There's no one in my life now who's just trying to stick their hand in my pocket. It's really a joy. That goes for everybody, from my travel agent to the band, to my publicist, and my manager. I'm very, very lucky to have a such a team and I really firmly believe that you get what you deserve. You get what you ask for.

I feel like I've made progress in terms of cleaning up my house, as Swamiji used to call it. I've gotten better mentally, physically, spiritually. The people around me are a huge part of that and I'm proud, really proud that I have this team. They call themselves "Team Felix" and I would be remiss if I didn't say once again that they're like family, the family I always wanted as a kid, along with the family, the kids and grandkids that I now have.

The Italian, or Mediterranean, tradition teaches you that it's your family who is most important; they are the ones who will look out for you, but that's not necessarily always true. There are others. I'm really blessed to have people like my friend Tommy, who I talked about earlier, in my life. Let me tell you, he's been a friend since I was a boy. His mother took over and helped when my mother passed away. She knew what I was going through, and she was there for my sister and me. What can you say about people like that? They've always been in your life and

are still in your life. You're fortunate if you have good people behind you; you're way out in front, no matter what comes at you.

For a while, in the 80s, I didn't have a manager. That's been true a number of times throughout my solo career and a lot of things just didn't turn out as well as they could have. Now, I have Obi Steinman, who is the best manager anyone could have, mainly because he cares. A manager, first and foremost, has to understand the business of music, but he also has to care. When you meet somebody like Obi who has the foresight and the vision to say, "Okay, here's what you got to do. You got to make sure people know your name. You can't go around thinking, *oh, I know I'm so great and everybody will know that.* You've got to tell them." You can't tell people yourself how great you are; you need somebody else to help you do it. Publicity costs money and your manager needs to convince you to spend that money to let the audience know you're still out there; without that, it's not really going to happen. That's one thing Obi did for me.

Another is helping me with having a proper presence on stage that demands and commands the income that you're asking to get. You can't go out there looking like a $5,000 group and demand $25,000. It ain't gonna happen. The easiest way to sum it up relates to how I first met Obi.

It was at the IEBA music convention in Nashville. My agent at the time, Steve Peck, set up a lunch meeting with Joel Brandis, who I believe managed War and Family Stone at the time. Obi was there for the Lebanese food. I felt bad that the conversation went from Joel wanting to manage me to Obi and I talking about food, politics, books and sports. Obi had indicated that he was tired of working with hard rock groups and planned to take a break from artist management. He just was burned out with having to baby sit. As our lunch continued, Obi looked up and said, "You know it's really good to see an artist with a brain."

I replied, "You know, it's really good to meet a manager with brain."

After lunch, I called Steve Peck from my car. I asked if he thought Obi might be interested in managing me. "Hold on." He handed Obi the phone and said, "Felix wants to speak with you."

"It was great meeting you. I had a blast at lunch. Would you consider managing me?"

"It was an honor to meet you and I would love to manage you."

In one of our first brainstorming meetings Obi asked one of those very simple questions that take a while to answer. "What's your plan? What does Felix Cavaliere still want to achieve in his career?" One thing that really hit me about Obi was his planning. His father would tell him you have to plan your work and work your plan. I told him I preferred to hear his plan. His pitch scared me at first, he really was introducing some radical changes.

But we began mapping it out. "Felix's wish list." I told him everything I still wanted to accomplish: A Christmas album, a Christmas touring show, playing with symphonies, writing this book, produce a new live show, revamp my touring business, increase my song writing, new albums, revamp and expand my publishing business. At this time, I believe that we have accomplished everything on that original list except my own wine label. However, that's still going to happen!

Since that day, one of the best things that ever happened to me in my career has been Obi Steinman. He's part of my family now. He's got my back. I often tell people that if I had Obi managing my career 50 years ago, I'd be in a very different place financially today. I'd probably be writing this while sitting on my own private island. The point is you have to have people who are looking out for you, for your best interests, not their own. The Beatles had a phenomenal manager; Led Zeppelin had a phenomenal manager. Foreigner had a phenomenal manager. You can't be a super group without a super manager. You need someone steering the ship; you can have a great ship, but if no one's at the helm guiding it through the rough seas, where are you? Either up on the rocks or sunk down below.

Like I said previously about guys like Sam and Dave, real pioneers of soul, who made songs like "Hold On, I'm Coming" and "Soul Man," they never made any money. They made all this great music, but no money. To this day, my friend Steve Cropper goes out on the road with the Blues Brothers who play all over the world, copying those songs and bringing in a lot of money; Sam Moore, the only surviving member of Sam and Dave, doesn't make any of it. That's a tough reality, but that's the music business. You can't turn around and say, "I hate this business; I hate the people in this business." You don't want to get to that point. It doesn't help to be cynical or become bitter. You have to realize the business of music isn't about the best work getting the biggest reward. Unless you've got some business sense, you're in trouble. It's got nothing to do with the quality of the work. You've got to put your ego aside. It's not about honesty, integrity, and all that. It's more like learning the lesson in the lyrics of the Madonna song, "Living in the Material World."

It's all about the team, not just great management, and with Obi leading the charge, we've put together a team Felix that's been in place for several years now. I have an amazing PR team headed by the very talented and caring Melissa Kucirek. I've been blessed to work with great agents over the years, and for the last eight years, we've been represented by Jim Gosnell and his team at the Agency of the Performing Arts (APA). My responsible agent is Christianne Weiss, Vice President Head of Adult Contemporary. Christianne is one of those people who are just great to be around. She and Obi have worked beautifully together, planning my tours and enhancing my brand.

My name, Felix, says it all. I'm a really lucky guy. I'm still working. I can't complain. I just want to keep on creating as much as I can for as long as I can. I have a recording studio in my house. I still enjoy the writing process and am continuously motivated by the people I'm able to work with. These days, though, that's the way music is done. There may be five guys writing the same song, but they're seldom even in the same room. In fact, they hardly ever are. There's no actual collaboration. That's hard for me. If you're just sitting down writing songs by yourself and for yourself—the way they do it these days—that's tough for me. I like to collaborate. It's my nature.

I still have so many things on my bucket list, and in the last few years, many of them have become a reality. For example, on June 20, 2018, I fulfilled a dream. I was invited to do a show at the Schermerhorn Center in my adopted hometown of Nashville. It's a beautiful symphonic hall, and yes, I was finally going to play and hear my music with an entire symphony orchestra—one of America's finest, I might add. It was an evening that I know would have made my parents proud. It was the complete circle, from classical to rock to symphonic. A marvelous evening! My friends and family from all over the globe came in, and I appreciated every one of them being there.

As Frankie Valli told me that evening," You are going to have a ball and will want to do this again and again." He was absolutely correct, and I hope to be playing many more events with a full symphony orchestra.

This particular opportunity came the year before when I heard the Nashville Symphony play two magnificent pieces one weekend and was invited to the conductor's dressing room. It was phenomenal. Now I've been backstage in many places, including the symphony, but this was backstage with the conductor, in his dressing room, basically where he lives for the whole musical season. It was really an honor. He was the nicest guy I ever met. His name is Gian Carlo Guerro. I can't begin to tell you just what a great person Gian is; he shared so many stories of his world, and it was nothing short of phenomenal.

Preparation for playing with a symphony was time-consuming and expensive because, first, you need to have special charts written for the songs, to accommodate all the instruments in the orchestra. In the end, it's all worth it. Hearing your music played by a full symphony is very, very special.

I've never strayed far from my classical roots and having had the Nashville Symphony opportunity is such a major extension of my talent and ability. But that's what I love about new opportunities. They give you a chance to reinvent yourself and, if the music business hasn't taught me anything else in the last half-century, it's that you have to be ready and willing to reinvent yourself.

So much has happened in the last few years, and it's truly amazing and gratifying.

Another milestone was playing two shows in Hawaii back in 2017.

Hawaii has always held such a mystical, magical place in my life. I remember visiting Ohau with my father a couple of decades after his service there in WWII, performing with the Rascals, waking up on my lanai one magical morning, and penning "It's a Beautiful Morning." The magic of this paradise further motivated the writing of "My Hawaii."

It was while playing this song in Hawaii in 2017 and being blown away by the crowd's response that I so truly and deeply felt that if at 75 years young I still felt so much love and spirit from audiences throughout every performance, I wanted my old band mates to feel such love at least once more before we completely closed the chapter.

My first call was to Gene. He listened and his first words were, "You're right. We can't take any of this for granted anymore." I believe what he meant was that tomorrow's never promised, and he felt like me that one last go-round could be special. We decided one last

"RASCALS" Tour, a run of dates to say thank you to the fans, to show our fans the gratitude they deserve for being with us all these years. Maybe we would do three shows: Hawaii, Los Angeles and New York. It could be something special: three shows to finish our story.

We received an offer of $200,000 for one show in Hawaii from a special friend, "Uncle" Tom Moffit.

My next call was to Eddie Brigati to ask if he was interested. I told him about the offer and hoped that he, too, felt the tug, the pang in his heart for one last little run, just us and our fans, a re-kindling of one of the great loves of our lives.

"No, I have too much on my plate," said a nervous Eddie." He said he was planning to perform his lounge act at the Cutting Room in NYC. Bummer!

That left Dino Danelli. Dino was Dino, in my opinion, always having to be difficult. He would not discuss it over the phone. He insisted on having a face-to-face meeting in NY. The pang of that wondrous heartstring was immediately replaced with that old, here we go again, downer feeling that few other than Dino can deliver like a punch to the gut.

But Gene and I obliged and traveled to NY and met with Dino at his favorite Italian restaurant. An odd pungent smell hit me as I walked in the door. I was no longer hungry.

My goal—Gene's as well—was to have managers and agents work out all the business to allow us to simply play for the love of our music and our fans. To Allow my old mates to once again and for the last time the connection, that special irreplaceable togetherness that I felt with the fans that evening in Hawaii.

The three of us sat down and had a little fun. I enjoyed talking with Dino and Gene. After about 30 minutes, we called Obi back to the table. And Dino's attitude changed, he admitted to us that he hadn't played his drum set in several years. In fact, not since Nov 29th, 2013, the last show we did. He complained about a few health issues but eventually agreed to the tour after insisting on having a decision on the songs, the band, and marketing. I left there saddened and in doubt that the tour would ever happen.

Obi, my manager, took a picture of the three of us as we left the restaurant. He showed it to me as we were driving back to our hotel. That pang! I became instantly saddened at that probably being the last time the three of us would ever be together again.

As Dino walked away, Gene began to cry. He turned to us and choked on the words, "My brother Dino is not doing good; he is not healthy. He can barely walk across the street."

It was a dreadful process, involving months and months of negotiations. Gene and I agreed to most of Dino's demands. However, it was never good enough and Dino kept moving the goal posts. In fact, one of the biggest issues was that he did not want a majority rules voting process. He wanted his vote to count twice in case Gene and I voted against his idea. He wanted the agents to go get all the offers before he would even sign an agreement.

Dino's demands grew stranger and more incoherent. Have you ever dealt with someone who, instead of being up front and forthright, chooses to create an environment so incendiary that it's destined to explode? That, unfortunately, seemed to be Dino's path, ultimately sealing the fate of any future concerts.

In the end, Gene and I thought Dino knew he was unable to perform and just wanted to blow the tour up, actually demanding to be paid to stay home. I found that interesting since he resigned from the group in 1973. Saddened but undeterred, Gene and I chose to write our own closing chapter with a last run of dates in 2018. We put together a great band including legendary hall of fame "Special guest" Carmine Appice on drums.

The sound was inspiring. Here was the band playing and the audience connecting, spirits soaring. I can't tell you how wonderful and heartening it felt to look over and see Gene doing his thing. It was so close to how I imagined it that evening in Hawaii several months earlier.

And then came the seventh of September. Our seventh tour stop. We were in a lovely venue, the Alberta Bair Theater in beautiful Billings, Montana. The first song on our set list was "Midnight Hour." The crowd was great. So locked in. First songs are so often the barometer of how a show's going to go, and it was apparent to all of us on stage that this was going to be a great set.

We began the lead-in to "Beautiful Morning." And just like we'd done a thousand times before Gene and I turned toward each other, made eye contact and smiled. Only this time, instead of seeing Gene Cornish's smiling face, I witnessed his body lying on the stage floor. He had collapsed, I thought he tripped on his guitar chord or something, but it wasn't until I saw Obi running across the stage—I can still hear his voice echoing in my head, swirling around in my mind— "Call 911, call 911, get a defibrillator."

A strange, controlled hell had broken loose. It's one thing seeing a loved one pass out. It's a completely different matter watching a lifelong friend, a beloved brother having chest compressions performed on him. Obi and Mark Weber, our production manager began CPR aided by a retired nurse who jumped up on stage from the first row. All of this while a horrified audience looked on. There was a silence that engulfed the theatre. I remember hearing the sounds of people crying, the murmured sounds of people talking in soft, almost whispering voices, all while hearing the hellish sounds of a loved one's life trying to be kept alive.

By the time paramedics had arrived, the audience was being escorted out. Gene had been defibbed a total of 7 times. It was on our 7th show on the 7th of September. Someone upstairs was looking out for Gene as everything came up 7's.

On Oct 22, 2019, I had the pleasure of being inducted into the Musicians Hall of Fame in Nashville, my adopted hometown. This is an amazing organization that was created to honor the musicians who have made a contribution and impact to the music that has shaped our lives.

Many of the people who played on the records we all grew up on were honored that night and it was an unbelievable thrill to be among them. It was presented at the Schermerhorn Center in Nashville, the same place where I played with that great symphony orchestra the year before. It was a fantastic array of inductees, including Don Everly, Steve Wariner, the Memphis Horns, the Muscle Shoals section, Alabama, and others. To share a stage with the legends, plus Garth Brooks, Brooks and Dunn, Ricky Skaggs, Jason Aldean to name a few. I was so humbled that friends, family and fans traveled from all over the world to witness my induction.

Again, it was an evening I'll never forget. Paul Shaffer did the induction for me, and the evening was magnificent and heartwarming. Billy Joel sent a wonderful video on my behalf, which I truly appreciate. It was a wonderful event and another indication of the respect that is given to musicians and songwriters in Nashville.

I must also thank my parents again for sacrificing everything to make sure my sister and I got the best education, MAKING me take those PIANO lessons. Pushing me to be the best I could be. THANK YOU, MOM AND DAD because of you, your kid made it to the Musicians Hall of Fame.

Before the COVID pandemic, I was averaging 45 to 50 live shows annually all over the world. When music venues were shut down by COVID, I spent much of 2020 and 2021 working on songs for a new album and, like us all, adjusting to this "new normal," which included having to move or cancel more than 100 shows. It's the first time in my almost 60 years of performing that I was forced to take time off. Being away from my band and our fans was tremendously difficult for me. I really had to work to keep my mind, body, soul and voice in condition.

In 2021, we began live performances again unfortunately, the Delta and Omicron variances had other plans and our shows and mainly our target audience were forced to stop again. Through this pause, I've been doing so-called "master classes" on-line for musicians, ZOOM performances, live stream concerts, interviews, corporate speaking, and in October of 2020 we were thankfully able to get out for a few days to play an outdoor show at the Pala Casino, in California in October of 2020.

It's 2022 now and I'm 79 years old, my family is healthy and happy. We are so blessed! I see the light at the end of the tunnel, we have many shows booked and I am so excited.

Besides family, nothing gives me more pleasure than connecting with the FANS. The music means nothing without the greatest fans in the world. SO THANK YOU for such blessings and for being a part of this amazing journey.

Happily, I have continued to work and play my music for almost 60 years! I keep looking forward to the next chapter. It gets better and better.

And, above all, I'm still Groovin', and not only on a Sunday afternoon.

God Bless,

Felix

"Before Felix came along "an organ was something you had in your living room and you polished it, you didn't play it."
    --Tommy James of Tommy James and the Shondells

"When I first saw Felix play, I said to the other guys in our band, 'we're really going to have to practice a lot everyday just to get anywhere near that good' "
    --John Sebastian of the Lovin' Spoonful

"When it comes to the Hammond organ in rock and soul music, Felix was the pioneer. He's still the template"
    --Paul Schaffer, former band leader for the David Letterman Show

"Felix has that star magic of being able to fill a room all by himself"
    --Bruce Morrow, rock and roll radio legend

www.ingramcontent.com/pod-product-compliance
Lightning Source LLC
Chambersburg PA
CBHW071806080526
44589CB00012B/709